# SORCERER'S HANDBOOK

21ST ANNIVERSARY – COLLECTOR'S EDITION

MERLYN STONE'S UNDERGROUND CLASSIC

# SORCERER'S HANDBOOK

## A COMPLETE GUIDE TO PRACTICAL MAGICK

by Joshua Free writing as Merlyn Stone
with the original Foreword by Myrddin Wolfe

*Published underground by Merlyn Stone in 1998.
Revised and expanded to present this
21st Anniversary Edition.*

**JOSHUA FREE**
publishing imprint

© 1998 – 2019, JOSHUA FREE

ISBN : 978-0-578-55367-2

*"A Book That Changed The World. . ."*
*The original underground occult classic*
*Sorcerer's Handbook of Merlyn Stone*
*returns—revised and reissued—for*
*a special 21st Anniversary presentation.*

# —TABLET OF CONTENTS—

# SORCERER'S
# HANDBOOK

# FOREWORD TO THE REVISED 1999 EDITION OF MERLYN STONE'S UNDERGROUND "SORCERER'S HANDBOOK"

*by Myrddin Wolfe*

SORCERY.

The very word conjures to mind our images of "*magick*"—from the classic Merlin, to today's modern stage magicians. In the deep recesses of our imaginations, "magic" and "sorcery" have always fascinated the human race. Is it any wonder that here at the end of the 20th century our society turns back toward all things *magickal?*

I began my magickal education while attending college. Little then did I realize, so was a young boy who would later write the volume you now hold. Yet, my first brush with the enigmatic "Merlyn Stone" did not come until later. While looking through a New Age catalog one day, I spotted the ad for his debut work, *The Sorcerer's Handbook.* The ad spoke about how the book "told it all without the usual occult jargon." That was its biggest selling point for me, so I quickly purchased it.

When my copy arrived, I was pleasantly surprised. Not only did it fulfill my expectations—it surpassed them. *The Sorcerer's Handbook* presented many facets of occult knowledge in plain, easy to understand, language. Best of all though, *it made magick practical* for even the newest student.

I was, however, in for one more little surprise.

*"Merlyn Stone,"* it seemed, was only a high school student when he wrote the book I held. I was floored! How could a mere teenager understand this much of the occult, much less write a book about it? Luckily, I got the chance to ask him about it! He had included his web address and email address in the book—and being ever so curious, *I wrote him.*

I had to know how someone so young could pull this off. And That is when I was able to discover just what type of person *"Merlyn Stone" really* is. Although young in body, he is quite mature in mind—beyond description—someone that modern magickal practitioners would call an *"old soul"*...*"ancient."* And he clearly represents a new breed of millennial magician —someone who dares, no matter the odds.

This volume you now hold represents a milestone of achievement—a revised expanded edition of *The Sorcerer's Handbook* enhanced with new material and clarifications drawn from his other works. This book is quite simply the pinnacle of all things "magickal" and "practical" in the New Age—a beacon to shed new *light* on "magick"...the *light of practicality.*

...And may it shine throughout the new millennium.

*Enjoy it—and happy reading!*

—Myrddin Wolfe
Samhain 1999

# ORIGINAL 1998 EDITION INTRODUCTION TO THE MERLYN STONE UNDERGROUND "SORCERER'S HANDBOOK"

*by Merlyn Stone*

As I gaze at the bookshelf before me, I wonder what a century of New Age literary contributions has really accomplished. I see 1000 pages of Agrippa's *Occult Philosophy*; the Kabbalists *Sefer Yetzirah*; a million words comprising theosophy's *Secret Doctrine*; not to mention the brick of paper composing a *Complete System of Golden Dawn Magic*; and volume upon volume inspired by the same, shared by other esteemed authors such as Aleister Crowley or Kenneth Grant. . .

The available material is unending and providing for a ceaseless pursuit round-and-round the mulberry bush. . .

Humans certainly are engulfed with information in this "age of enlightenment," but what practical work comes from all this knowledge? It seems strange to me, that what I have already accomplished alone—and with assistance of a select few during my short life so far—already supersedes the work of those content in only knowing the academics of magickal theories and concepts of metaphysics. These "bookshelf sorcerer's" have never *known* true magick—never felt its true power running through their veins; they are content to just talk about it, even impressing a great many people. . .as the monkeys chase the weasel. . .round-and-round again we go.

"Magick" is <u>not</u> a bi-monthly newsletter, a fancy society, organization or weekly class. It is *Life* itself—and all that makes up existence. Every day, each person in this world faces the building blocks of magick. But, the "*sorcerer*"—a term chosen for this book regarding operators of magick of any gender—retains an upper hand, because they can recognize the patterns and acknowledge these facets as they truly are, using them to manifest the world as desired.

A "*sorcerer*" seeks to unlock the *secrets* of the Universe, questioning human-fashioned truths of the "world" to transcend the animalistic nature of *homo ferox*—literally "*man, the ferocious*" as coined in T.H. White's "*Book of Merlyn.*" The sorcerer may essentially do and become anything. It is this removal of trust and attention from abstract deities and concepts, placing it rightfully with "Self" that allows such an actualized being to be potentially the most powerful "system" functioning on the planet. . . *and potentially the most dangerous.*

Since the dawn of history: astrologers, magi, high priestesses and priestly wizards have been the true "*Guardians*" of this Earth. Sumerians, Babylonians, Celts, Egyptians and Greeks of ancient times all give evidence of this by their spiritual traditions. We look at it today and call it myth, but it was certainly *real* to them—and what has changed? What will historians say even of modern society in a far and distant future?

Who has read the *Old Testament* and not noticed the tremendous magickal powers of Moses? And also of the mystics who aided the Pharaoh...? And was it not by occult sciences that Persian Magi were led to the Christ-child? And what of the occult mysteries embedded in the religious ceremonial transformation of water into wine? True alchemy or a fabrication? And yet still today, the orthodox religions have forbidden the "*lay person*" from learning their birthright of magick!

Magick is a friend who seeks embrace, not fear. It is the girl-friend—or boy-friend—who is always there when you wake up in the morning and always returns your *calls*. As they say: *to know her is to love her*. Magick need not be honored as a religion, but is validated by true religion: as the theosophists say: *there is no religion higher than* truth, and practice of magick requires purification, research and dedication—not worship.

—Merlyn Stone
Summer Solstice 1998

# THE 21ST ANNIVERSARY INTRODUCTION TO "THE SORCERER'S HANDBOOK" COLLECTOR'S EDITION

*by Joshua Free*

During the 1990's, public interest in *magick* and *occult* subjects exponentially rose to new heights as few could have anticipated. The amount of "New Age" material published *soared*—the companies and creators that produced them even had the ability to, for the first time in contemporary history, develop both significant followings and legitimate income—or perhaps the other way around.

Now, someone reading this is going to quickly argue about all of the "developments" that they may have experienced in the 1960's, and further back still, we have witnessed a blossoming of occult lodges, which became most publicly visible during the early 20th century—factions such as the *Golden Dawn* and hermetic schools of *Theosophy* that are now over 100 years old since their founding. I am certainly not going to deny the existence of these things—but lets face it, the occult revival has only just recently passed its infancy, and that is why it has had so many growth spurts, though it still exists to simply test its own limits and get a feel for its skin... This is all changing now—existing in the ever-shifting *face* of reality.

I appeared on the "New Age" scene—however much "underground"—in 1995 as "Merlyn Stone." As I have explained to others along the way, the name was chosen for personal reasons and not as a tribute to the female author (Merlin Stone) of whom I had not even heard of at that time. My research had revealed that "Merlyn" is not even really a proper name. Although it has been used to refer to particular figures (or *a* figure) in history, it is actually a title—a *Welsh title*—that is best equated to a *seer* or *prophet*. The name even equates to "*Nabu*" in Babylonian—a name I also go by in some circles.

During only the three decades of my current existence in the physical realm I have watched as "crystal healers" went from working in basements in the 1980's to having fully leased and store-fronted offices. I have watched as the thousands who once only reserved themselves to secluded monthly meetings using back-entrances from dark alleys and the study of books in closets by candlelight, now wear their full regalia in public places reserved for large festivals and parades.

Don't get me wrong—I understand that many of you have endured suffering still to this day for your inclinations toward a "mystical," "occult" or otherwise "pagan" *living philosophy*. There are still more who are unable to exist in this freedom I have just described, worried for the very real repercussions and animosity that can come from work or family—lives in this *system* can be lost or laid to ruin. Believe *me*, I fully *understand*. But... times are changing *still*.

The heights of the 1970's and early 1980's really paved the way—cushioning the *societal* blow that often comes with large "paradigm-shifts." Among these, of course: the Simon *Necronomicon* that appeared in 1977—the same year as *Star Wars* and the birth of the *Shannara* epic by Terry Brooks. Mainstream consciousness was being upgraded, and naturally the *guise* it took form as was usually always something other than what it *appeared* to be as is often the case in the "material realm." While more obvious introductions of semantics were born from *Dungeons and Dragons*, and related *fantasy* enthusiasm, the children of the 80's were also being prepped—their minds opened to new realms of possibility that were veiled in the paradigms of their parental generations.

In the past, I have even referred to various pop-culture mystical and magical themes coming into focus with the cult interest in such aspects as *Dark Crystal*, *Care Bears*, *Labyrinth* and the like. To the extent of my experience, however, it was 1995 that provided the most paramount shift. I took a step back, observing the wide-angle, and it was not difficult to see rising prominence and mainstreamed influence of the newly released motion picture *The Craft,* coupled with a more family-friendly *Sabrina the Teenage Witch* as the featured "after-school-special" of the day. Clearly the coast was clear and it was time to emerge—and come *awake!*

While I was most certainly not alone in hearing the "call" to awaken, the work I had to do—and the *program* I was here to follow specifically—was not something readily communicable to, or understandable by, the population at that time—even a "New Age" one. The plans were laid before I even showed up in this life, but patience was key, as was the constant vigilance for signposts of a path *never* traveled. Mostly it involved me keeping my head down—It was going to take everything to bring the outer work to its heights and the format it is now presented as—but in the 1990's, the world was not ready for what I had to say concerning the origins of "magick" and the "Mardukite" legacy. So, I had to start at the beginning—to build a basis—and work from a foundation rock-*stone.*

All of my original writings related to the occult field—including the recently revised and reissued "*Draconomicon,*" "*The Druid's Handbook,*" "*Elvenomicon*" and the current version of "*Sorcerer's Handbook*" which you now hold—were originally the result of private "in-house" materials prepared for working study groups and research oriented societies that I was personally involved with—and often, in part, the "founder" of. When I consider that I began this work publicly in 1995, it is now nearly a quarter-of-a-century later and the work has *evolved*—taken many forms—though in the beginning, it was easiest for me to reach my own demographic: *esotericists, occult practitioners,* and up and coming *NexGen alien youth* that usually carried natural inclinations toward "New Age" topics.

In 1995, the world was not ready for *Mardukites.* I worked within the paradigms that were much more accessible and did not require a lot of "background"—*ritual magick, spellcraft, high psychology* and even *ceremonial* systems.

There were two methodologies I was most concerned with, which connected directly to later work that I hoped to accomplish—and which is now known or branded "Mardukite" —primarily the "*Pheryllt Druid*" material of Douglas Monroe and also "*Simon's Necronomicon.*" But, this was about as close as I could come to "mainstream New Age" facet interests, and these two specifically had been enshrouded in misguided controversy and restricted recommendations from the more "publicly elite" and visible organizations and their leaders. "Members" of well known groups were explicitly told *not* to look into these materials—just as much as my modern *Mardukite* work has seen its lion share of fallacious scrutiny and disapproval from the uninitiated.

From 1995 through 1999, I assisted in producing not only several ritual collections—or "Book of Shadows"—for practicing underground groups, but also led my own operating and experimental social circles, teaching workshops and lectures in local Denver-area New Age outlets and bookstores. One of the popular workbook companions I developed for this later expanded into the infamous *Sorcerer's Handbook by Merlyn Stone*, with additional materials now collected in our appendix of *Lost Books of Merlyn Stone*. Some of these later notebooks and contributions were commissioned strictly for private use by small groups—but even all these twenty-one years later, records still remain, and for posterity, I have decided to include many of them for this twenty-first anniversary presentation.

This legacy, as accounted for in former editions, begins when the *Sorcerer's Handbook* made its underground premiere in 1998. The "first edition, first printing" was printed from an old-fashioned typewriter—reproduced and bound by a local Denver printer, until one day they decided to actually read it... then they refused to bind it anymore. After circulating for a few months, a second edition was printed exclusively for members of the Elven Fellowship Circle of Magick and the Order of the Crystal Dawn, two interconnected underground occult organizations in Colorado using the text as a primer

"Book of Shadows" for their outer circle membership. It was, however, the third edition that some people might be familiar with—circulated into the thousands—after the title was picked up by Abyss Distribution/Azure Green from 1998 until 2001 when it went out-of-print synchronous with "Merlyn Stone's" *disappearance.*

Simultaneously revolutionary and introductory in its delivery, *Sorcerer's Handbook*—and early works such as *The Druid's Handbook* and *Draconomicon*—served as inspirational precursors to materials I later developed more thoroughly in order to establish the "Mardukite" brand of occult interpretation, including *Elvenomicon* (formerly titled *'Book of Elven-Faerie'*), *Arcanum: The Great Magical Arcanum* and remaining volumes of the 'Mardukite Core'—such as *Necronomicon: Anunnaki Bible* and so forth. It is due to the wider circulation of my more recently developed work that interests revived regarding early contributions and distant origins.

Over two decades after the fact, I am pleased to present these works for returning fans and the next generation in a format prestigious enough to give true commemoration to the legacy of the *Sorcerer's Handbook of Merlyn Stone*—incorporating elements from all editions since produced, public and private —the end result: a collected works anthology of all surviving "Merlyn Stone" materials beyond even those restricted to the original *Sorcerer's Handbook* proper—making this perhaps the finest edition of the *Handbook* ever to be released.

Whether you've come for the instruction or the nostalgia, I hope you will enjoy the journey. . .

*. . .into the discovery of the magick.*

—Joshua Free
Lughnassadh 2019

# SORCERER'S HANDBOOK

# THE CORE OF MAGICK

It exists in all things and is likewise the driving force behind all magick. Whether something is living or not, it has energy, a force that can be changed and manipulated by the will of the *"sorcerer."* Energy cannot cease to exist—nor can it be created. It simply *is*. But constantly it revolves and abounds —changing form. The *"sorcerer"* is one who seeks to recognize the patterns of Cosmic Law in play and use them to manifest change in accordance with their will—to *be the cause.*

Symbols are merely substitutions of solids. All of the actions, words, symbols and dramatic enactments performed in ritual magick are meaningless without the proper knowledge and experience regarding energy "currents." Energy required for magick is everywhere around us—in the very fabric of space and the most miniscule seed of life—although invisible to the untrained eye. Sorcerers therefore learn to recognize this energy, to channel and even harvest it--for personal gain and/or societal improvement. More than a special religion or cult-following, "magick" is a "paradigm"—a holistic way to view the world and interpret life based on its energetic qualities.

There are two main sources of energy utilized in magick, which are actually one and the same—but processed differently. Firstly, there is our "personal power"—the energy that enables one to physically walk, sleep, study, think. . .*and yes*, even have sex. This energy may be raised for magickal purposes through mental concentration, using focus/attention/awareness, and by activating muscles in the body—such as we do unconsciously when we are emotionally charged.

All personal states—that we are led to believe result from the world at large—are generated or produced internally. Therefore, the Sorcerer learns how to properly manage these states and maintain personal conscious control over them. This energy is directed as currents (or "rays") to any source to affect energetic/subtle change based on the intensity of our focus and attentions.

The second source of processed energy is external. Very often in "natural" magick (earth-oriented systems), this second source is considered *Nature-power* or "earth power." In high magick and ceremonial systems, this power may be called *celestial* or "cosmic power"—as aligned to a specific figure, the astral plane or another dimension (or perceived level of reality) that is communicated with—and all energetic interaction *is* a communication, and all existence is one in wholeness.

Power of a *sorcerer* is then only limited by one's imagination—or more importantly, ones ability to visualize and imagine. Through acts of ritual magick, the *sorcerer* can raise personal power, merge it with external powers (which are called forth or summoned) and direct it with the "mind" via visualization. "*Visualization*," as we are told, "*is the key to the occult.*"

### "MAGICK" -vs- "MAGIC"

Aleister Crowley once said:--"The whole question has been threshed out and organized by wise men of old; they have made a science of life complete and perfect; and they have given to it the name of *magick*."

The primary reason (Crowley's numerology aside) for accepting a change in spelling is to create a distinction between the practical occult "magickal arts" and the illusionist "magic" and parlor tricks used by those only *pretending* to manifest overt occult powers for entertainment. Both spellings are accepted in "New Age" literature.

## VISUALIZATION

Key to the process of magick is the "art" of visualization. This is an innate ability to create images and pictures in the mind. Problems on the physical plane are often created (and even resolved) from the process of "visualization." Its mastery is a mental power or skill, which enables the Sorcerer to gain a certain degree of control over the physical world—and when the mind is operating on the body, an emotional somatic or discharge of chemicals ensues.

Basic visualization-based rituals follows a formula:

> 1. raising energy
> 2. visualizing the change occurring
> 3. sending energy to the cause

Thus is the bare bones of ritual magick—enabling one a direct energetic means to *be the cause* of change more rapidly then when left alone. We are not forcing tides—we are riding the waves. In magickal terms, this is "channeling and harvesting energy and directing it to a desired target to affect a change."

"Visualization" is the primary faculty allowing us to maintain conscious control over the total Self using innate and internal communication with "imagery." These skills allow you to observe changes as if they have already taken place and put attentive energies into these images. All intended change actually works on this principle: a person first sees the desired change in their mind and then acts. *Action follows thought.*

## CEREMONIAL HIGH MAGICK

This style of magick is used by adept Sorcerers in order to manipulate the mental and spiritual planes. The magick energy discussed prior is sufficient for "manifesting" on the physical plane—in the mundane world. But everything is connected, and the same rules apply, but more are added. High magick delves deeper into complexities of systems, ceremonies and ritual aids representing abstract spiritual concepts.

Magick using spellcraft, witchcraft and the like for purposes of affecting physical change is not "high magick." High Ceremonial Magick is specifically used and mastered in order to achieve transcendental states, erupting from the belief that humans have a potential for more than the restrictions that material systems portray. The "New Age" has revived beliefs drawn from mystic folklore, cultural charms and spellcraft, but the craft of wizards was also passed down by a different stream.

Some traditions of "high magick" are also considered "holy magic"—noted for their particular alignment to "*priestly*" systems representing the "Great Work," accessed by methods not otherwise focused on the manipulation of the mundane world. Priests of the ancient temples served as intermediaries between "gods" and the general population. When people brought requests to the temple, the priests supplemented their prayers with powerful invocations and religious ceremony, thereby also affecting the consciousness of the people, their world-views of reality and belief-based energetic interactions with the universe.

## CONCENTRATION & THOUGHT DISCIPLINE

In addition to the ability to visualize concrete imagery, the Sorcerer must also possess concentration skills and thought discipline. "Thought magick" requires the mental faculties to hold a clear image in the mind for prolong periods of time. This is where most novices will usually require the most personal development to execute effective magick.

Begin by sitting comfortably and allow your thoughts to drift for several minutes. First, go through what you were thinking and cause (or will) it to be replayed as precisely as possible. Next, allow your thoughts to drift and then still your mind, holding one thoughtform in your head for as long as you can. Don't strain, but focus on a single thought. If your mind begins to wander, gently correct yourself and begin to focus on the thought again. The final step is to keep the mind completely clear of all thoughts for as long as possible. Practice with these basic techniques is essential to gaining the necessary discipline over the mind.

"Relaxation" is critical to concentration and meditation—the ability to gain and keep a relaxed state of inner peace at will. Of course, not all magickal practices require the same state of mind, but absolute clarity in your focus is essential, including self-control and self-discipline, particularly concerning emotional energies. Such workings where vibrant imagery will better aid magick, would of course, be nullified by "relaxation" for the entire duration, but without proper focus, the energy in the ritual can become "wild magick." Intensity is not the same as clarity.

Meditative states may be achieved by sitting or laying in a comfortable position where your muscles are free from tensing. When your muscles begin to tense or you get anxious, regulate your breathing and gently "will" your muscles to relax. Restlessness is fairly common to those who are not used to such "stillness." Proficiency in such skills will significantly prepare you for the magickal work ahead.

*Self-discipline comes from self-correction.*

As a final exercise of ability, try this:—Relax; clear your mind; then, make an intentional recall of a specific recent event, consciously replaying the same stretch of information from memory, capturing as much of the original details as possible. Reproduce all of your original emotional involvement and stimuli: visual sights, physical sensations, sounds, smells, and so forth.

Experiment further by "projecting" your observational perspective into different aspects of the scene—see if you are able to examine a specific detail more closely than you had at the time of the event or perhaps you might recall an expression or reaction of someone else that you had noticed prior.

If you do not find blatant success with these techniques at first, don't stress. Gently try at it some more as you continue your development through this book. These are basic methods toward personal empowerment that appear at the heart of all ancient magical and mystical systems of education.

## BREATHING

Rhythmic breathing is a prerequisite for most magickal work as part of the initial grounding process—which is not always indicated in an "advanced" ritual text. With experience, this process becomes automatic, as do visualization skills. Proper "controlled" breathing is not only important for your physical well-being, it also affects your ability to meditate, relax or energize your body and aura—called "energy work."

During deliberate breathing exercises, oxygen should be inhaled via the nose to slow and warm it through the sinuses. Fix your tongue to the roof of your mouth closing it off as pull air in—you should even be able to hear its passage.

Mystical work involving energy (which is practically all of it) is enhanced by proper breathing—distributing air throughout the personal energetic system of the total body. When you breathe in, you can feel the energy flowing into your pores and flowing through the body. By adding visualization imagery, you can project a conceptualized idea (or polarized energy stream) into the area around you and even interact with it (*e.g.* breathing it in, or exhaling it into the environment). This stream of energy is directed by *emotional charge, concentration, will* and *attention*.

Rhythmic breathing means conscious gauging of breath. As you "count" specific intervals, your breath should be steady and maximized. Completely fill and empty your lungs, some-times holding in between—based on the exercise. This can be uncomfortable at first, but eventually it should yield a sensa-tion of mild euphoria—as it is amazing what proper breathing can do. One popular method we call "quad-breathing," count-ing four seconds or heartbeats for each part of the cycle: breathing in (counting to four); holding (counting to four); exhaling (counting. . .); and holding.

## WILLPOWER

It is imperative for a Sorcerer to maintain a true sense of self —in absolute *Self-Honesty*. The Sorcerer must always be in control of the body and mind—must always have control over actions and thoughts that ensue from said body and mind. This is called true "willpower" or "self-direction." As such, the Sorcerer maintains a higher sense of personal responsib-ility—the *ability-to-respond*—over energetic interaction taking place between Self and the Universe—which at the highest and truest level of interconnected (entangled) existence is one and the same: All-as-One.

Routine practice toward developing personal willpower may seem awkward at first—often pushing yourself to think and behave in a manner you are not normally accustomed. That is to say: don't allow clocks, schedules and impulsive "desires" to rule your life. When feel impulsively hungry, tired or in-clined to naturally react in a specific way, challenge yourself to control your behaviors and ultimately the outcomes of your actions. See if you can manipulate these sensations or transform them into something else.

This type of work might seem trite to some or will be open to misunderstanding by others, so let me clarify: this is not to say to deprive yourself of food and sleep or to carry around false emotions and reactions. The intended goal is to learn the causal patterns of these reactions—and in turn, how to be *more* than a "reactive" individual, and to learn to actually "act"—to create sequences of active energy that are in line with one's actual goals and in conjunction with Cosmic Law. This type of training is also designed to increases one's conscious control over the body—because after all: How can you transcend the physical body, if you are bound by it?

# MAGICKAL CORRESPONDENCES

*"Magickal Correspondences"* are based on the ancient occult concept that: *like attracts like energies.* The various lists that follow are similar to those found in many New Age "how-to" occult books. They document observed symbolic representations that may enhance personal vibrations during ritual.

Is it an absolute requirement to follow these for effective magick? No—*but,* they are decent "fine-tuning" devices when using "ritual magick" *systems.* The basic lists given are "universal"—they comply with a consensus of accepted ancient source texts and traditions—but personalization is also a requirement of magick, so they may be amended so long as the Sorcerer has an educated personal interest in doing so for increased effectiveness.

### LUNAR POWERS

Even the word "month" is semantically connected to the Moon's cycle. This can be measured in either "sidereal" or "synodic" periods. A sidereal month is approximately 27.3 days and marks the time for the moon to physically complete an orbit around the earth planet. Synodic months account for the simultaneous rotation of the Earth and marks approximately 29.5 days. Together, these figures give us an "observed" lunar month of 28 days. There are ancient lunar calendars dating back to the Sumerians and Babylonians of Mesopotamia that also possessed 29 to 30-day *"luni-solar"* months.

Even before the science was properly understood, Sorcerers long believed that the moon maintained a significant impact on our earthly lives and on the planet itself. Since magick is generally oriented toward "Nature"—or the "Universe"—the effect of the moon on mystical work influences many modern magickal traditions and traditional icons of the same—the archetypal *lunar goddess*. The ancient Sumerians simultaneously gave the moon male attributes, as the Anunnaki god *Nanna*.

Magickal workings and performances may be gauged to the proper times of a lunar phase in order to add the lunar effect to a ritual. Different lunar phases impact in different ways. Of course, it is not always possible for a Sorcerer to wait for the proper lunar timing to perform a magickal working.

> The *Full Moon* is a "psychic high-tide." It is the strongest time for invocation spells that draw or attract something towards you. This could be love, protection, healing, &tc.

> The *New Moon* is a time for darker workings—those workings which deal with the secret and hidden.

Ceremonial and ritual texts will often indicate if either the new or full moon is favorable. A second new moon in a single month is called the *Dark Moon* and is thought to be even more powerful than a regular new moon. Likewise, the second full moon in a month is called the *Blue Moon*.

The *waxing moon* is a period between the new moon and the full, when the moon is perceived to be getting larger. Since the light is strengthening it is a perfect time for invocation magick—that which draws something to you.

A *waning moon* falls between the full moon and the new, when the moon is perceived to be getting smaller. Many view this as a time of purification and banishing—when focal energies are warded away.

## PLANETARY POWERS

Planetary influences are a reoccurring theme in magickal notebooks and *grimoires*. Each day of the week is "ruled" by a specific celestial planet and these influences are coupled with lunar phases to gauge the timing for many spells and rituals of material interest. Many *grimoires* catalog their hierarchy of spiritual entities based on governing planets—a tradition that extends back to Babylon—which also correlates with favorable timing for ceremonial communication.

---

### Planetary Magick & Days of the Week

SUNDAY—*Sun*—Leadership, sacredness, success, power, God, solar observations, change and fire.

MONDAY—*Moon*—Faerie magick, psychic/psionic development, Goddess and the water element.

TUESDAY—*Mars*—Courage, protection magick, military endeavors and victory.

WEDNESDAY—*Mercury*—Communication, mental, development, divination, intellect, air element.

THURSDAY—*Jupiter*—Animals, business ventures, celebration, force, expansion and wealth magick.

FRIDAY—*Venus*—Arts, beauty, fertility, glamour, growth, love magick and the earth element.

SATURDAY—*Saturn*—Banishing, binding, curses, hidden influences, initiation and secrets.

---

## COLOR SYMBOLISM

Colors play a significant role in affecting perceptions of the mind. When looking at any color—specifically large blocked spaces like walls or colored-paper—you will see that colors make you "feel" a certain way. Experiment with each color in the spectrum by making cards to correspond. Using your intuition, "feel" the color energy of the cards with your eyes open, and again with your eyes closed. The next step is to attempt to "feel" or "intuit" (distinguish) colors of the cards without looking. Of course, this is only a suggestion.

Energy streams (currents and rays) and auras are often distinguished or interpreted based on color. The candles, altar dressings, robes, talismanic squares and amulet stones that appear throughout magickal lore are often included due to their color associations. For example: red candles used to draw love or black altar dressings to banish evil, &tc.

---

### The Color of Magick

WHITE—Purity, truth, healing, full moon; *Monday.*
RED—Passion, sex, love, strength, courage; *Tuesday.*
ORANGE—Power, healing, success, attraction; *Thursday.*
YELLOW—Communication, mind, confidence; *Sunday.*
GREEN—Fertility, renewal, Earth, fortune; *Friday.*
BLUE—Tranquility, peace, understanding; *Wednesday.*
PURPLE—Wisdom, psychic, spirits.
BROWN—Money, business, animals, the home.
GRAY—Cancellation, stalemate, neutrality.
BLACK—Banishing, hexing, loss, evil; *Saturday.*

---

**KEYS OF MAGICK**

The first ingredient is *desire.* It is imperative that a Sorcerer truly desires the result of the magick with total *Self* in order for energetic change to occur more rapidly. The purpose of magick is to ensure the outcome of what one *desires.* Beyond mere "wishing," you must *desire* something deep enough to move the energy—and ritual operations can compliment this.

Desire alone does not create change—*timing* is also important. The target of the energy being moved should be most receptive to the magick: Plans must be executed in proper sequence and personal targets (humans) are most easily influenced in their sleep (or at night) when the subconscious is most active. Any "planner" can tell you that improper *timing* is one of the most detrimental facets to implementing any goal.

*Visualization* and *imagery* allow one to peak individual imaginative processes. Focusing energy on a representative image—also called "sympathetic magick"—allows proper direction of energy far more than simply calling out a name. In magickal workings and other types of energy work: *like forces attract like forces.* There is a reason specific colors and forms are suggested in various effective ritual texts.

Energy raised through ritual and intention must have a specific *direction.* Anxiety and any other lack of emotional clarity will detract from desired results. It is actually quite common for novices to worry about the success of their workings. Understand, however, that dwelling on the energy spent may keep that energy localized or fixed on you when it should be released (directed)—"rippling out"—into the universe. Rather than physical actions producing or yielding undesirable or unseen results, the Sorcerer directs energy in an unseen way to produce physical results. These results can take some time to manifest or "condense" in the physically perceived world.

---

THE ELEMENT OF AIR

Direction – *East*
Rules – *Intellect, mental, thought, knowledge, wind, mountaintops, fields, clouds, vapor, storms, purification, new beginnings.*
Time – *Dawn*
Season – *Spring*
Color – *Yellow (purple)*
Zodiac – *Gemini, Libra, Aquarius*
Tools – *Wand, incense, visualization*
Fragrances – *Frankincense, lavender, rosemary*

Faeries – *Sylphs, sprytes, pixies*
Animals – *All birds*
King – *Paralda*

---

## THE ELEMENT OF FIRE

Direction – *South*
Rules – *Creativity, change, transformation, flame,
    destruction, volcanoes, sexuality, passion, energy.*
Time – *Noon*
Season – *Summer*
Color – *Red (green)*
Zodiac – *Sagittarius, Aries, Leo*
Tools – *Dagger, sword, staff, candles*
Fragrances – *Orange, lime, citron*
Faeries – *Salamanders, fire-drakes, the phoenix*
Animals – *Snakes and reptiles*
King – *Djin*

---

## THE ELEMENT OF WATER

Direction – *West*
Rules – *Emotional, feeling, intuition, love, fertility,
    oceans, rains, wells, cleansing, dreams,
    subconscious, sleep, psychic.*
Time – *Dusk*
Season – *Autumn*
Color – *Blue (orange)*
Zodiac – *Cancer, Scorpio, Pisces*
Tools – *Chalice, cauldron, mirror*
Fragrances – *Camphor, lemon, lily-of-the-valley*
Faeries – *Undines, merfolk, sirens, naiads*
Animals – *All fish and marine life*
King – *Niksa*

# THE ELEMENT OF EARTH

Direction – *North*
Rules – *Physical body, nature, foundations, solidity,
   success, money, death, forests, trees, animals, crystals.*
Time – *Midnight*
Season – *Winter*
Color – *Green / black (white)*
Zodiac – *Capricorn, Taurus, Virgo*
Tools – *Pentacle, stones, salt, herbs*
Fragrances – *Sage, pine, ceder, cypress*
Faeries – *Elves, gnomes, dwarves*
Animals – *All four-footed*
King – *Ghob*

# BASIC TECHNIQUES

## THE MAGICK CIRCLE

All ritual magick is performed within the confines of a "magick circle." Such working areas are realized in various ways depending on the tradition or system used—some in circles of trees (called "*groves*") or in circles of stones (called "*henges*"). Some ceremonial magickal *grimoires* suggest the use of flour or chalk to mark the physical boundary of a circle on the ground or ritual chamber—even suggesting the use of two, or in some cases *three*, concentric circles.

The purpose of the magick circle—literally "*mandala*" in eastern traditions—is to keep energies raised within the circle, "in" the circle, and protect against energies of the outside world. The circle, when used for a magickal working, is called a "*nemeton*"—meaning "sacred space" in some European traditions. This area should only be used for magickal workings, mystical studies and meditation.

The location of the *nemeton* is up to you—in most cases, it will be dependent on your means. In medieval times, some wizards devoted entire rooms, towers and dungeons for these activities. More natural earth-oriented practitioners operate outdoors to best communicate with "Earth power." The size of the circle itself depends on the location and the number of participants using the *nemeton*. Sufficient space should be dedicated to these purposes—allowing for an altar (if used) and other ritual tools, not to mention the free motion of energy and activity. Solitary practitioners often use their own height as the diameter; then adding three for each additional participant involved in the ritual.

Circles are a powerful geometric symbol—one of the most basic universal shape-forms—next to the square, triangle and cross-pattern. Esoterically, it equates with perfection, unity and recursive-infinity. The circle resonates a feminine polar vibration, typically representative of the water element on Earth, or the *Cosmic Sea* of *Infinity* extending throughout all existence. Somewhat ambiguous in "New Age" terminology, a "circle" may also refer to a group fellowship or "coven" that frequently gathers at the sacred area, *nemeton* or "circle."

The circle is the most sacred and prominent symbol found in all of sacred geometry—which is, in effect, *all* geometry. The Sumerians and Babylonians first divided the circle into 360 degrees for their religious beliefs long before it was understood in classical mathematics. Immediately after this, the Egyptians began making calculations for what the Greeks termed "*Pi*," starting with *256/81*—or *256*-divided-by-*81*. This calculates as 3.16(04938...). Most modern students are aware of the close approximation used in c. 250 B.C. by Archimedes as "3.14"—derived from 223/71, and the Babylonian 22/7.

## CASTING A CIRCLE

Every system, tradition and grimoire—from the highest form of ceremonial magick to the most primitive rites of shamanism—practitioners operate rituals from within a sacred space, deemed *consecrated*. In most instances, this *nemeton* is represented by a "circle"—even if that circle is squared or divided by any number of other geometries. There are megalithic examples throughout Europe such as Stonehenge—and even the Native Americans used a "Medicine Wheel" to observe their cosmic rites. The sorcerer must fully acknowledge that this ritual space exists apart from "ordinary" mundane reality as a representation of the ALL.

The ritual circle is a *microcosm* of the Cosmos. It may also be squared to four directions defining the "ends" of the material or elementally manifest Universe—often called *Watchtowers*. The four "quarters" are recognized as elemental thresholds or wards governing the four planar spatial directions around us: north, south, east and west. [Activities of "above" and "below"—the *net* interaction or *"wave-form"* of energetic exchange—is treated specifically by the operator themselves.]

In ritual and ceremonial magick, these four elemental directions are represented by specifically colored candles, tablets, banners and other appropriate symbols. The ritual tools—also called "elemental weapons"—represent movement of energy, its action and motion—each corresponding to an appropriate elemental vibration, tone or frequency. The Sorcerer uses the objects during rituals consciously and intentionally as a focus instrument, symbolically and energetically linked to the very manifestations that they represent. In this way, a ritual circle simultaneously functions as a *macrocosm* of the otherwise internalized realm of the mind, dramatically played out using symbols and abstraction in the place of solids, to promote or induce a creative state of *being* and *doing* that mirrors the emotional, intellectual and energetic interaction taking place with a world of solids—thereby creating a *reality experience.*

The circle is traditionally distinguished by a physical boundary or marking—many grimoires suggest natural substances such as chalk, flour or salt. Visualization is also employed to better fix the energy of the circle in consciousness. Advanced examples—given later—are known as the Rituals of the Pentagram, but even these preliminary rites are used for a practice referred to as "casting the circle." When a physical circle is not clearly marked or physically defined—perhaps other than a basic representation of the four quarters—visualization is even more critical. It is easy, however, even if for only temporary use, to use a staff or sword to physically trace a circle boundary on the ground when practicing outdoors. In either case, after the physical ground-level circle is defined (or not), a mental/astral boundary is traced and visualized in space using the wand or another tool aligned to the air element.

While tracing the circle, the operator projects a ray of light energy, which forms a protective band. Traditions differ regarding the colored-band involved: some indicate using clear or white light; others suggest whitish-silver; and many of the modern magickal revivals of the late 1980's and early 90's use blue. Some practitioners skilled in the use of visualization in ritual will go as far as to see this light band extending above and below the ceremonial space as a "sphere" or "egg." Keep in mind: the key to a successful circle casting is recognizing the distinction between ordinary space and sacred space, and then by incorporating rituals that selectively demonstrate the entangled interconnectedness of that space with the ALL. In effect, the magick circle represents the chessboard of the Sorcerer's reality game. The "pieces" are put in place during a manageable predetermined ritual setting—and just before the end of the working (or energy play), this reality is projected ("uploaded") into the Universal Consciousness.

While performing ritual magick, a Sorcerer is affecting the Universe by intentionally projecting energies stored up—perfected and refined—within the *nemeton*. People actually affect reality everyday with their energetic interactions of emotion, thought and action. The Sorcerer dedicates their practice to learning to more effectively manage this energy—and with more disciplined faculties and focus. Nothing "supernatural" is taking place—it is all within the domain of "natural law."

The most basic methods of circle-casting require only visualization and energy:—Go to the eastern quarter of your circle and use your index (power) finger on your projective hand (the one you write with, or right hand) and draw the boundary of the circle as you walk clock-wise or sun-wise (to the south, &tc.) and return again to the east. This completes the mental/astral boundary of the magick circle. The esoteric key is to charge your projective arm with personal energy and release it through your finger as you mark the boundary. When the energy is visualized "whitish" or "blue," the magick circle may qualify as an energetic "circle of protections" or "COP."

Practitioners will often opt to have an "elemental" (colored) candle or beacon burning at each cardinal direction. When appropriate the most traditional colors are:

| | |
|---|---|
| East – *yellow* | South – *red* |
| West – *blue* | North – *green* |

Candles, banners and tablets that represent these elemental directions aid the Sorcerer in focusing their awareness and communicating properly with each of the energies in ritual. Most paradigms of ritual and ceremonial magick follow this four-fold elemental schema of "*Gates*" or "*Watchtowers.*"

To provide an example of a circle-casting group liturgy, the following ritual text is derived from the "1998 Book of Shadows" used by the Elven Fellowship Circle of Magick (EFCOM). This script features only the dialogue of the ceremony—with each direction represented by an individual coven or circle member—requiring practitioners to already possess familiarity with the energetic work and visualizations required for an effective circle-casting. This specific example calls forth proto-Druidic primary energy currents of "Awen" and "Menw," incorporates key elements of the Chaldean "Watchtower Ceremony" and other European lore of Tuatha d'Anu tribes.[*] It may also be supplemented by any additional ceremonial rites and/or ritual steps (e.g. calling elementals).

---

### *Casting the Circle—Group Liturgy (v.1998)*

East: "We consecrate this circle of power to *Menw* and
    *Awen.*"
South: "May they hear our calls and bless us with power."
West: "May the Elder Gods, the Shinning Ones, aid and
    protect us."

---

[*] See also *"Elvenomicon -or- Secret Traditions of Elves and Faeries"* by Joshua Free.

North: "We stand at a threshold between worlds in a veil of mystery."

East: "*Oh-roh Ee-bah Ah-oh-zod-pee.* In the names and letters of the Great Eastern Quadrangle, I invoke thee spirits of the Watchtower of the East."

South: "*Oh-ee-peh Teh-ah-ah Peh-doh-keh.* In the names and letters of the Great Southern Quadrangle, I invoke thee spirits of the Watchtower of the South."

West: "*Em-peh-heh Ar-ess-el Gah-ee-oh-leh.* In the names and letters of the Great Western Quad rangle, I invoke thee spirits of the Watchtower of the West."

North: "*Moh-ar Dee-ah-leh Heh-keh-teh-gah.* In the names and letters of the Great Northern Quad rangle, I invoke thee spirits of the Watchtower of the North."

East: "May the forces of the Watchtowers be present among us."

South: "Let us now conjure the powers of the Masters."

West: "And may with their powers come the wisdom to use it."

North: "From the northern city of *Falias*, I summon Master *Morfessa*. Bring the Stone of *Fal* and stand as Guardian of the North."

East: "From the eastern city of *Gorias*, I summon Master *Esras*. Bring the mighty Spear of *Lugh* and stand as Guardian of the East."

South: "From the southern city of *Finias*, I summon Master *Uscias*. Bring the Sword of *Nuada* and stand as Guardian of the South."

West: "From the western city of *Murias*, I summon Master *Semias*. Bring the Cauldron of the *Dagda* and stand as Guardian of the West."

North: "May the powers of the Four Masters be gathered here among us."

## CALLING THE ELEMENTALS

After the circle has been cast, Sorcerers may call on the elemental beings that dwell in Nature and on the astral plane. Sorcerers often incorporate this ritual step into their circle-casting rites. If a communicable relationship is established, "elemental beings"—the intelligences of the elements—may aid the Sorcerer in magickal workings as powerful co-magicians—and should be treated with respect.

---

### _Calling the Elementals (version 1998)_

• Go to the East and proclaim:

_Ye spirits of Air, Elemental Sylphs of the East. I call thee here now to aid in the magick I shall perform. So mote it be._

• Go to the South and proclaim:

_Ye spirits of the Fire, Elemental Salamanders of the South. I call thee here now to aid in the magick I shall perform. So mote it be._

• Go to the West and proclaim:

_Ye spirits of the Water, Elemental Undines of the West. I call thee here now to aid in the magick I shall perform. So mote it be._

• Go to the North and proclaim:

_Ye spirits of the Earth, Elemental Gnomes of the North. I call thee here now to aid in the magick I shall perform. So mote it be._

---

Using the magickal key of "visualization" you can see an elemental being of proper elemental traits coming to the edge of your circle from the given direction. It should be made clear that when called forth properly they are present, but the Sorcerer may need to initiate a communicable energy exchange using willpower and visualization. By engaging in this over time, experiential rapport or "authority" may be earned with the elements and "kingdoms" within their energetic domain.

## CALLING DEITIES

After the elementals—and other spirits—the Sorcerer can call on any personal deities or archetypes to aid in the magickal working. Some of the more religious systems of magick have adopted sacred pantheons drawn from the Celts, Norse, Egyptians, Romans, Babylonians, Sumerians, Greeks and the like. Virtually every culture has a similar celestial or planetary mythos that may be utilized in magick—each a part of an authentic religious tradition specific to that culture. Wicca is one modern example that traditionally evokes dual powers of a "god" and "goddess"—as relayed in the following example, conducted in the circle before images of the deities.

---

The Call to the Goddess:

*Goddess of the Starry Skies, Goddess of the Fertile Plain,*
*Goddess of the Oceans Sighs, Goddess of the Gentle Rain.*
*Hear my calling to you this hour.*
*Open wide the Gate of Mystic Light.*
*Waken me with your graceful power.*
*Aid me in my magickal rite.*

The Call to the God:

*Great God of the Forest Deep, Master of the animals and Sun.*
*Here in a world lost to sleep,*
*now that the day is done [just begun].*
*I call to you in the ancient way, here in this circle round.*
*I desire my will to be displayed*
*and I call you to send your powers down.*

---

## CLOSING THE CIRCLE

The sorcerer shows respect for the energies and entities that are called to the magick circle. This etiquette is a significant facet of ritual magick and the establishment of communication channels with these energetic intelligences. At the end of a rite, it is customary to work the preliminaries backwards: beginning with the thanking and dismissal of the "god" and "goddess" (deities); followed by the elementals; and then the "extinguishing of the circle."

For the elementals: go to the north and dismiss them at each direction in turn, counter-clockwise to the west and so forth. Ask them to return promptly to their place of dwelling but to come again to your aid when called. After this, the last necessary part of ritual magick is extinguishing and grounding the energies used to cast the circle. This may be accomplished in multiple ways. Some go to the north and travel the boundary of the circle (counter-clockwise) using the receptive hand, re-tracing—and retracting—the energy band ring. Alternatively, a Sorcerer might ground the circle by standing in the centre of the circle with arms upraised, visualizing energy of the circle being sent down, deep into the ground... deep...deeper —down into the fiery center of the Earth to be recycled and transformed. This is often literally called "grounding."

## RAISING ENERGY

During magical operations, the Sorcerer is responsible for properly handling ("channeling") the mystical cosmic energy that enables thoughts to manifest in the Universe. Remember that ritualism ("spellcraft") and ceremonial magick are all a combination of internally produced and externally generated energies. Using only your own stores of personal energy will leave you feeling drained, possibly depressed and more susceptible to magickal warfare—via a weakened aura. On the contrary, channeling only overtly powerful raw external energies without tempering/filtering with your own personal energetic system will result negatively or as wild magick. The best way to understand this is to compare the idea to electricity. External power transmitted to your house is unusable without first "stepping it down" with a "transformer," which offers the same "energy potential," but alters the voltage to something conducive to your power needs at the outlets—*e.g.* 400,000 volts down to to 120 volts. Using personal power alone would be similar to draining a battery or auxiliary generator without supplementing it with external power sources.

The ability to properly raise energy is paramount to the success of magick. In all personal developmental systems and apprenticeships, the skills of energy use are among the first practical lessons encountered. The process of raising energy draws on the most fundamental skills—breathing techniques, grounding, visualization, thought discipline and willpower— and applies them directly for constructive personal use. The seeker will find such applications of energy used in casting a circle or raising a cone of power during initial phases of ritual workings. The *nemeton* is conjured with personal energy and becomes your metaphysical catalyst or "transformer" for the external energy that is called in—*e.g.* elementals, drawing down the Moon (or Sun), dragon-calling, Enochian Magick, Goetic evocation, &tc.

Traditional Wicca, neodruidism and even the new Mardukite brand of Mesopotamian Neopaganism all seek to revive archaic pantheons of "old religions" so that these traditions can be remembered and observed today. Most revivals of specific regional-cultural systems work from a "table of deities" comparable even to the powers of the saints called upon in Catholic rites and Santerian rituals. Whether integrated into ritual spellcraft or a seasonal/holiday/festival celebrations, those practicing a "system" aligned to a particular culture will call on names and powers of appropriate "archetypes" from within that pantheon. For example, when raising energy for love magick, the operator may also call forth energy from a deity of corresponding to love from that pantheon—such as Aphrodite (*Greek*), Isis (*Egyptian*) or Inanna-Ishtar (*Mesopotamian*), which are in fact all the same figure! Yet, the cultural diversity found in the New Age has even led to formation of eclectic systems that blend pantheons and call on all multicultural representations of an aspect. This is okay, so long as the practitioner is fully aware of the symbolism and tradition behind all of the deities and pantheons incorporated.

Raising energy can be a challenging part of the magickal process. Not only is it crucial to success of ritual workings, it is also often difficult to properly relay and learn from New Age books. Chanting, singing, drumming and dancing (music in general) are all commonly used in shamanic and indigenous Nature-oriented systems to draw a swelling power within the *nemeton*. These activities promote muscle tensing, absorbing and storing a cumulative draw of energy in the physical body.

Variations on the muscle technique may include visualization of an "orb" or "ball" of energy that your form between your hands. Personal energy and external energy is pushed into the "energy ball" and then directed (released) via intention. The "*Middle Pillar Rite*" from the Golden Dawn System—given later in this volume—also helps raise energy for high magick by activating the *chakras*—or "personal energetic system."

Before practicing any energy work—such as raising energy— perform preliminary grounding and relaxation methods that you find necessary to bring your total conscious mind to a "magickal state." This is easier to achieve with practice. Then conjure your *nemeton*—which is practiced on a mental/astral level without performing a physical ritual. While seated within—begin rubbing your palms together, back and forth. Begin slowly at first, then progressively increase the rate. As you do this, you may notice that the muscles in your body naturally becoming tense. As you continue to do this you feel energy swell and accumulate. When you feel the energy peak—before you are going to slow down—stop and pull your hands a few inches apart. Focus your attention between them and then slowly move your hands apart and then close together, repeatedly in slow sweeping motions. You may see and feel the energetic "orb" or "sphere" manifesting before you. Charge it with your intentions—via "visualization"—and focus any external bands—or "rays"—of energy into it; then release it to the Universe, carrying energetic intentions of your goal to the "Akashic Records" and back again to manifest. Take note of the personal energy used during the process. You may feel fatigued afterward, so eat a light meal and rest.

## AUTOSUGGESTION

Magick involves the subconscious mind—the part of the human brain that automatically dictates or interprets reality for your conscious thought. It is within the power of the subconscious mind to utterly change perceptions of reality. This has an affect on global or universal consciousness, which is a shared reality among humans—the game parameters that we agree to. The intensity of our thought influences others by our perception of reality if they are effective and powerful.

Traditional lore suggests that the subconscious is at its most receptive—or active—state during sleep. Therefore, whenever dealing with magick intended to influence others directly, it is suggested to perform workings when a target is sleeping. If the energy is moving quickly enough, it may have an effect on their subconscious immediately during performance.

The subconscious stores the information that we "believe," which we make real every day—manifesting into existence—and finding validation for everywhere we turn to reach the degree necessary to make it *real*. Humans are programmed to believe that they are dependent on certain habits and systems—socially and methodically conditioned—but by going beyond these and into the programming of the subconscious, reality is actually affected and *true magic* happens!

## THE THREE SORCERER ARCHETYPES:
## SEX, SENTIMENT & WONDER

SEX – Sorcerers who are blatantly sexually appealing and exceptionally charismatic. They are enticing and beautiful—and tend to rely on such traits in exclusion to all others. They use their looks and sex appeal as a powerful weapon on others, but this can just as easily be turned on them if they are not maintaining control of game conditions.

SENTIMENT – Sorcerers who are generally eccentric and live the "village witch" and "hermit" lifestyle. Their enchantments and enigmatic nature, sometimes bordering on whimsical, may offer mystery to children and adults alike. They are stereotyped versions of archetypal witches, wizards and magicians from "fairy tales." They have herbs, candles and incense well-displayed, and obscure esoteric trinkets everywhere to capture the eye.

WONDER – Sorcerers who extensively take time to alter their physical/outer appearance to maintain a particular "glamour" or aura in all interactions with the "world-at-large." We are, of course, speaking of the most obvious examples of "Goths" and teenaged vampyres—but also those others that will openly apply their magical prowess to public awareness. In modern society, they are what we have come to expect of the "wizarding folk," including black dressing, heavy make-up, altered hair-styles and any other outward indicators that these individuals are "walking the walk."

# MODERN WITCHCRAFT & WICCA TRADITION

In 1951, Anti-Witchcraft and Anti-Magick Laws were repealed with public practice no longer punishable by imprisonment (or death). Previous underground magickal organizations and secret societies sought to perfect "ceremonial magick"— such as the "Hermetic Order of the Golden Dawn"—and publicly visible figures like Aleister Crowley were already considered "witches." Intensive revival interest in witchcraft tradition occurred in the late 19th-Century and early 20th-Century in-dependent of the ceremonial elitists, claiming descent from more rural folk-oriented mysticism, emphasizing gypsy folk magic, the ancient Celtic "fairy-faith" and goddess worship.

Three influential literary works appeared in 1890, which set the stage for later Wiccan, neodruidic and neopagan move-ments of the early-to-mid 20th Century "proto-New Age."

—*The Golden Bough*, written by Sir. James Frazer; a monu-mental treatise classifying many diverse folk or "pagan" traditions and customs, with a particularly emphasis on Nature.

—Samuel MacGregor Mathers translated the notorious grimoire, the *Keys of Solomon*. Initial interest was limited to fellow Golden Dawn (GD) members, but it later became a staple of ceremonial magick practice and even Wicca.

—Charles Leland, a historian of gypsy and Italian-Strega traditions, published *Aradia: Gospel of the Witches*, presen-ted as a secret tradition connecting covert underground witchcraft movements since the 14th Century.

In 1921, an anthropologist and Egyptologist named Margaret Murray, author of *The Witch-cult in Western Europe*, investigated the works mentioned above. This is what sparked Gerald Gardner's revival of witchcraft in the form of "Wicca," drawn from an old Anglo-Saxon root meaning "wise" or "wild." The tradition, and the *Book of Shadows* used to found it, received input from two other figures seldom credited with it: Aleister Crowley and Ross Nichols. The tradition borrows heavily from ceremonial and ritual magick, occult correspondences from *The Keys of Solomon* and *The Magus*, native European "Old Ways," the "Gypsy" and Strega traditions of Eastern Europe, coupled with Celtic, Druidic and Norse mysticism from Western Europe.

Where neodruidism, the Rosicrucians and most magickal organizations and secret societies were predominantly solar (Sun) oriented, Wicca aligned its system to the Moon with an emphasis on the "goddess," a focus that is not found extensively in Medieval and Renaissance magickal styles. Gardner's tradition—called "Gardnerian Wicca"—also promoted skyclad or nude work within covens. In the 1960s, Alexander Sanders ("Alexandrian Wicca") became a self-proclaimed "King of the Witches," leading an alternate Wiccan tradition that placed a heavier emphasis on ceremonial magick and grimoire use.

Many of the facets found in the the overall system are quite old, but those who subscribe to the New Age eclectic tradition of Wicca are practicing a system that was actually consolidated less then a century ago—giving rise to a thousand other traditions, obviously even younger. The lure of the magickal tradition—the ability to possess books of magick and don the wizard's cap—has captivated curious minds for centuries and seekers often discover this lifestyle by one means or another.

The great archetype of magick is universal, but it is also open to interpretation by cultural consciousness—its language semantics and processing by one's own individual psyche. The overwhelming inclination to pass manuscripts or ritual texts off as "older" than they are is an ever-present concern in all forms of mysticism. It is, however, counterproductive to personal magickal development to get caught up in a political whirlwind of origin and authenticity debates. Oral traditions and even personal (or family) systems have always operated in a mysterious manner and become even more cryptic when first transcribed into the written word. The esoteric or occult is what it is for a reason—often obscured and disguised before us in plain sight, but seldom recognized *en masse.*

Modern Witchcraft has been misinterpreted, according to the New Age, as merely a feminine alternative to "masculine wizardry." In Wicca, gender dualism is recognized. It would have to be, especially given that many prominent figures throughout its inception—Gerald Gardner, Alex Sanders, Raymond Buckland, Scott Cunningham, &tc.—have been male! The covens, however, appear to be led by a "High Priestess," who is considered spiritually superior to any male priest. There are even exclusive Dianic forms of Wicca open to females only.

Significant increase of interest in Wicca emerged in the mid-1990s, resulting from the motion picture, *The Craft,* depicting teenage girls, including Fairuza Balk, practicing magick as a coven. What is peculiar about this fad-appeal to Wicca is that the movie did not really depict Wicca so much as a Hollywood presentation of ceremonial and ritualized high magick. The "fictitious" grimoire used in the movie, *The Invocation of the Spirit,* is clearly a copy of Waite's *Book of Ceremonial Magic* (although the lightning-storm illustration does not appear in it, nor do any of the rituals the girls practiced in the movie).

In the 21st Century, "Wicca" has become a household catchall term for many aspects of the New Age. What is actually practiced today is minimally based on the work of "Gardnerian" or "Alexandrian" interpretations. Some aspects of neodruidism overlap into the varying Wiccan traditions and elements from all systems of magick, whether primitive shamanism or the *Sacred Book of Magick of Abramelin the Mage,* seem to be fair game. While some practitioners fault others for not knowing "their" version or vocabulary of mystic practices, too many variations exist to qualify one or another as a "purer" strain.

## COVENS, CIRCLES & GROUPS

Covens are a social unit from which Wicca and witchcraft traditions operate. Earliest reference to the term "coven" dates back to 14th Century Ireland. The semantics appear nearly synonymous with similar rooted words, "convene" and "covenant." The New Age has seen an arrival of larger "schools" and "churches" of these traditions, but the majority of practitioners rely on a smaller coven or family unit as a basis for operations. Covens generally operate completely independent from others, overseeing adherence to the main principles of belief without having to report to a hierarchical authority outside of the coven structure.

Traditionalists maintain a belief that true covens must have exactly thirteen members, the number of annual lunar cycles. Depending on the flavor of leadership, there may be twelve members and a "High Priestess" or a High Priest (*King of the Witches*)—or even eleven members and a leader of each sex. This is typical of "closed covens" or "family traditions" that do not openly invite membership.

At reaching thirteen members, a coven may opt to "close" their membership, or if necessary, have members leave to form off-shoot covens that best fit individual needs. Group magick is delicate and requires the right number of participants—and the right participants. Too few will not move enough energy and with too many it is often hard to focus energy properly on a single goal. By modern definitions, a coven is simply a group, whether study oriented or experimental.

"Training covens" will typically have two different "circles" or subgroups. The Outer Court or Outer Circle serves to initiate and apprentice novices with less than two years experience in a coven. Inner Circles are responsible for dispensing the teachings maintained by the coven and leading ritual operations. The Outer Court participates with the Inner Circle in all solar *sabbat* and lunar *esbat* observations. The Inner Court also comes together to "coven" independently of the Outer Circle, discussing the rites and formulas of their tradition and experimenting in advanced practices before members of the Outer Circle are introduced. Depending on the size and needs of a coven, *wyvern covens* may be established for the young.

Contrary to what many traditionalists may tell you, the coven is not a necessary part of the magickal life. There are actually far more solitary practitioners out there working from books, taking classes and inheriting traditions from past generations, than practicing magick in traditional covens. The craft term has also expanded to include other magickal paths not specific to the "religion" of Wicca. In fact, many general magick covens consist of Gnostics, neodruids, Norse-revivalists, Mesopotamian neopagans and even Unitarian-Universalists. The New Age movement has expanded awareness into diverse facets of knowledge, revealing that the heart of every ancient and indigenous culture contains some magickal tradition and interpretation of deities, Sky Gods, and avatar-like heroes they bred. A coven will typically align themselves to a specific cultural mythos and pantheon—though many eclectic covens also exist.

Novices are not encouraged to start their own covens. An individual may be powerful, even more powerful than an entire coven, but groups can move large amounts of energy quickly when properly directed. Having several inexperienced practitioners dabbling together unchecked is simply a prelude for an energetic catastrophe. When no coven is accessible, it is suggested that interested individuals form "study groups" to pursue the material academically before adding concerns of flashy "ranks" or "titles" and all of the other drama that can be associated with group magick and group hierarchies.

Members of the "study group" can come together to learn and discuss, experiment individually and then reconvene to compare notes. The purpose of a coven shouldn't be misconstrued as simply a vehicle for group magick. Covens may not even perform traditional "magick," coming together only to ritually observe seasonal *sabbats* and astronomical celebrations. These operations seldom connect directly with the type of archaic currents of energy that can get you into trouble. Group participation in "spellcraft" (ritual magick) on the other hand, may be challenging. All participants have to raise synchronous energy and direct it with visualization simultaneously. Therefore, the obvious recommendation is to perfect your magickal skills as a solitary practitioner before merging those energies with the "group consciousness"—and then be particularly careful *what* group you involve your energy with.

## GROVE FESTIVALS

There are eight traditional "grove festivals" recalled from the lore and mysteries of ancient Wizards, Sorcerers, Druids and Mystics. They mark specific times of year that have both astronomical and agricultural significance for planet Earth. They are particularly important in rural pagan traditions and for those who work and live in harmony with the earth ways. This current model of the "wheel of the year" is common in most contemporary neopaganism.

Traditionally the "new year" festival in the New Age is called *Samhain*—pronounced "sow-en"—and it is the original celebration of Halloween: the eve of October 31st into the month of November. It is a time in honor of the "dead names"—our ancestors—so dress up in your finest costumary and perform rites in the secrecy of the forest around a "bone"-fire.

*Yule* is the original pagan celebration of Christmas—a time in honor of the oncoming rebirth of the Sun "god"-child at the "Winter Solstice"—usually December 21-22. The "Yule Log,"

Christmas Tree, use of mistletoe, holly and ivy are all customs from the ancient Druids that have now been integrated into contemporary living.

*Imbolc* occurs on February 1st—now observed in America as Groundhog's Day. It is derived from an ancient candle festival also known in Western Europe as "Brighid's Day"—a time of looking forward to the coming spring. Customs include the dressing of corn dolls to ensure a prosperous spring season.

Spring Equinox is astronomical holiday equated with modern symbolism of Easter or *Ostara*—coinciding with the Babylonian "Akiti" New Year festival. As with the Autumn Equinox, the timing and energies of day and night are balanced—usually March 21-22—and the Sun enters the house of Aries, as plotted in ancient Mesopotamian astrology. Hunts for eggs, pastel colors and wearing of green clothing have all been handed down to us from the Celts as popular spring customs.

May 1st marks the major fire festival now called "May Day," but the ancients knew it as *Beltane*, literally the "Fires of Bel" —a primordial name for "Lord of the Earth." Bonfires are lit and the "maypole"—representing the "world tree" and link between the upper and lower realms, in addition to its more commonly known fertility symbolism—is erected and danced around. This is an observation of the spring season turning to summer.

The Summer Solstice, as many are aware, is the "longest day" of the year—the height of solar power annually. To this day we carry visions of white-robed Druids in procession, ascending hills to convene in stone circles to greet the morning sun at dawn—usually June 21-22.

*Lughnassadh* marks the beginning of the harvest season with the "wedding festival" of the Celtic stellar-deity, Lugh on August 1st. The height of a harvest is marked with the Autumn Equinox on September 21st, equivalent to our modern "sentiments" behind Thanksgiving Day—but without the aboriginal genocide. This was a time for the rural-pagan agricultural folk to give thanks to "spirits of the harvest" and the "spirits of the wine" and the "spirits of the grain". . . and so forth. Thus is the traditional neopagan "wheel of the year"—bringing us full circle back to *Samhain*.

## MAGICKAL NAMES

When you start to use magick, begin to address "spirits," or when you are initiated into a magickal circle, you usually will assume a new "identity-name" for these application that is to distinguish you from the "persona-you" that is brought to the everyday "mortal world." It is not uncommon for a person to take on several of these names for various purposes or social activities—"circle name," "secret name," *&tc.*

## RITUAL DRESS

Since the Sorcerer assumes a different "identity-name" to fit their magickal work, it only makes sense to replace "street clothes" for these operations as well—of course, sometimes this cannot be fully helped.

Then again—there are times when one just feels like getting decked out in black clothing, make-up, eye-shadow, chokers, cuffs, with all manners of crystals, talismans, dangling from every possible surface. This isn't *always* and it isn't for everyone, but when you are in the privacy of your coven—or even your own bedroom—you have a chance to explore the shadow side of yourself that also seeks embrace. Some Wiccans follow a bit of a departure from the norm on this—working *skyclad*, which is "dressed by the sky" or nude. Given that Gerald Gardner was a nudist, this comes as no surprise. It is clearly a matter of taste, but it certainly is not required—nor is it necessarily a gateway to ritual abuse.

## PRINCIPLES OF BELIEF

In 1974, a grand convocation of witches occurred (in Minneapolis), where Wiccan elders formed a council to unify a codex of doctrine or belief that could be met on a universal level. They numbered them as a series of by-laws and presented them in a straightforward fashion that would not be open to misinterpretation—summarized as follows:

PRINCIPLES OF BELIEF FOR NEOPAGANISM

1. Rituals are to be performed in accordance with Nature, the seasons and phases of the moon.
2. We seek harmony with Nature and believe in ecological responsibility.
3. All have the potential of magick, even if it is not outright apparent.
4. We believe that the creative force is dual, equal in both male and female aspects.
5. We acknowledge the outer world of the physical as well as the psychological realm of the mind.
6. We honor those who have wisdom to offer, but do not recognize an authoritarian system.
7. Religion, wisdom, witchcraft and magick are combined to form the "pagan way."
8. One is not a witch unless they live in harmony with Nature. The title alone is meaningless.
9. We believe in the continuation of life, the evolution and development of consciousness beyond this life.
10. We do not deny others the freedom to believe in their ways. They should respect ours.
11. The debate of the history of witchcraft and the terminology therein is not our concern.
12. We do not acknowledge the existence of an absolute evil or devil figure and therefore don't worship one.
13. We believe we should seek Nature for health, wellbeing and holistic medicines.

# THE ARTS OF SPELLCRAFT

Did you know that simply tying your shoes is an act of spellcraft or practical magick? Don't argue with me yet! Let us explore this subject deeper.

The basic act of "spellcraft" is intended to cause a change in accordance with your will—or to make something happen because you want it to. Thus, no matter the means, tying your shoes because *you* want them tied—and *you cause* this manipulated change in physical reality—*is* spellcraft! Of course, you don't think about it like this—we seldom realize that we are willing our bodies to move and act from a "higher state"—but that is essentially what is happening. If you *can* look at spellcraft in this way, however, you will find it very simple to master.

*But how exactly does a "spell" work?*

The circle is cast; energy is raised; the goal is visualized; and energy is released to that outcome. Finally, the circle is extinguished. Herbs, incense, candles, incantations, &tc. all aid in attracting proper energy. The *Key* to ritual magick, or spellcraft, as with other forms, is that "like attracts like" forces or energies. If, for example, you want to attract the energy rays of love and release this attractant-frequency of energy toward an outcome, then you will need to surround yourself with tools and aids that directly help you in attaining that specific energetic state. You may also use magickal correspondences provided throughout this current book to further supplement applications of this *Key*.

## SPELLCRAFT UNVEILED

"Spellcraft"—also called "low magick" or "ritual magick" in various texts, is the most common method of using the power of intention and willpower taught in the New Age. The purpose of this art is to learn to direct the energy of the desires and will of the operator through dramatic representations. Anthropologists even recognize this practice among indigenous shamans in the form of "sympathetic magick." Spellcraft is primarily concerned with influencing energetic change in the mundane/physical world levels such as fertility, wealth and love. The main tenet is that the currents of energy attached to you in the future are based on the raised energy and projection of emotion, thought and action in the present. Jesus said: "Ask and it shall be given; knock and the door will open." Sorcerers learn the most successful questions to "ask" and best means of "knocking."

Conventional spellcraft and prayer are essentially the same. Most religious practitioners are not instructed in the proper and most effective ways to pray, leaving them at the mercy of established organizations for any real "divine intervention." But Sorcerers do not wait for "divine intervention." You are the only one responsible for your own life. God has given you the mental and spiritual faculties to recognize the Right Way to Ascension. Through proper focus, emotional purity and intention of will, you can attract any ray of light into your life.

Remember that magick is the ability "to see any transformation manifest in the physical world in accordance with will." It does not matter what means are used: setting and meeting goals for change is a unique human faculty of awareness: you can affect the future by acting in the present. This is no small realization since it has allowed "human civilization" to rise. Following in line with the old masonic code, the truth is: if your intention is to see something through, it doesn't really matter if you accomplish this by some form of telepathy or simply some old fashioned hard work.

Hopefully, you are traveling the path of least resistance so as to apply the most appropriate energy type in the most appropriate way to accomplish all of your goals.

Ritualized spellcraft is operated very closely to practices of "ceremonial magick," but with more mundane ends in mind. Use of elemental tablets, elemental weapons, herbs, incense, robes and cloaks may supplement the basic formula of spellcraft. "Candle magick" is especially useful and constitutes an entire art in itself. Spells may be as simple or elaborate as you deem necessary. Additional tools and implements are only included if they actually help you to connect with the desired current/state of energy. They should be removed as distractions if they do not. For this reason a controlled environment, —whether hidden away in Nature or in a room dedicated to esoteric/occult practice—is most effective. Any unnecessary non-magickal distractions should be removed from surrounding space and *nemeton*. In some traditions of "high magick," ritual chambers are sometimes designed following specific parameters that are reserved for ceremonial purposes only.

Virtually every tradition in the "New Age" teaches the arts of spellcraft differently. Some texts include vague preliminary steps that a Sorcerer should have developed familiarity with prior to ritual attempts—such as those basic techniques and skills offered in previous chapter-lessons. An ability to be grounded, focused, use breathing techniques and enter the body of light are all paramount to ritual success before even beginning to "cast a spell." You may also wish to prepare graphic representations of your intention—pictures, symbols and talismans—so long as the Sorcerer is effectively connects these "representations" with the "actuality." Inability to do so accounts for many initial failures using "spellcraft." It is also possible to be too concerned with the ritual "text" and verbiage itself during operations, which will not keep the energy of your attention where you want it during the process. The formula for basic spellcraft is as follows:—

---

### The Sevenfold Spellcraft Formula

1. Casting a Circle (conjuring the nemeton)
2. Calling Elementals (summoning external powers)
3. Raising Energy (personal blended with summoned)
4. Visualization (seeing the change presently occurring)
5. Releasing Energy (see toward the change as present)
6. Dismissal of Spirits (closing ritual formalities)
7. Extinguishing the Circle (grounding residual energy)

---

Adepts throughout the ages have always advised their apprentices not to dwell on their workings once completed. It is a common mistake made among novices to worry about effectiveness of a ceremony. Once energy raised in a ritual has been consciously released into the Akashic Field or Universal Consciousness, allow it the chance to resonate and vibrate its own ripple effect. If you recall this energy back to you with your thoughts, it will not be "out there" working for you. One common suggestion is to sleep afterward and allow the subconscious mind to equalize and "catch up." This is not usually difficult since many spellcraft operations are best performed at night under correlative lunar and planetary influences.

## TOOLS OF THE ART

"Ritual magick" incorporates specific symbolic tools or implements into rites, which the Sorcerer must either construct or find. Most of them are attributed to the four elements. The Sorcerer represents the "fifth element" in the ritual, surrounded by and embodied by the "four." An Akashic Box or storage chest may also be used to store the elemental tools, which becomes a "fifth elemental" symbol of quintessence in itself—and keeps the tools from prying eyes. There are other "lesser" types of ritual aids that a Sorcerer frequently keeps a supply of, including various types of gemstone and consumables such as candles, herbs and incense.

*The Air Wand*—Whenever one thinks of witches and wizards the "magic wand" immediately is conjured to mind. More than purely a fanciful stereotype, the wand represents the "air element" in ritual and the action that follows thought. In folk traditions they are often made of wood, such as Hazel and Oak. Other tree-wand associations include: Apple and love; Ash and healing; Pine and prosperity; Rowan and protection; Birch and purification. The Willow is also a common wand-wood. They average about fifteen inches long and half an inch thick; placed to the east when inactive during rituals.

*The Fire Blade (Dagger or Sword)*—A "magick blade" represents the Sorcerer's sheet cutting will, force and desire during the ritual—representative of the fire element and placed to the south during rituals. Herbalists will also commonly have a separate knife used only for cutting plants, herbs and roots.

*The Cauldron*—Another common association with witches, the cauldron or alembic pot-still is indicative of alchemical transformation. It used for burning "fire-water" (alcohol) during rituals and/or brewing herbal potions and tinctures.

*The Water Cup (Chalice)*—holds drinkable liquids—water, wine and other libations and ceremonial mead during rituals. A "magick cup" (goblet or chalice) may be of any style, or from whatever materials seem fitting, are available (and, of course, affordable). Some Druidic elementalist lore refers to using a personal "shell-chalice" to represent water (in the west).

*The Earth Pentacle (Stone)*—is a circular plate of wood, metal, wax, clay or stone, six to eight inches in diameter and half an inch thick. Using sandpaper (if wood), the disk should be finely prepared and a five-pointed star painted or engraved into the plate with the tips reaching the ends of the disk (or a border line drawn as a circle around the disk). This is placed to the north as a symbol of Earth. Pentagrams are also a sign for the Self or Sorcerer as the magickal operator or quintessential "Fifth Element"—the *active observer* in the cosmos.

## MAGICK FOR OTHERS

Novice Sorcerers may find this almost completely unsuccessful. Spellcraft requires personal goals, intense emotions and true needs. The desire and willpower required must be genuine for it to be powerful. This can be adventurous enough for a person to access for their own benefit then alone the wants of another. If you do a "love spell" for yourself, then you fully understand the need and can feel the desire—and this create manifestation. It may be very difficult to sufficiently raise the same level of energy for the pure gain of another.

Sorcery and magick are powerful tools for one's own self-development and improvement. They are *tools*. Potentially, it is more beneficial to teach another the primary rules of spellcraft—or obtaining one's own personal goals—as opposed to attempting to "cast a spell" for them. There are also many ethical matters to consider as well, particularly concerning any "karmic" energetic backlash that may result from interacting with or influencing someones life.

## CANDLE MAGICK

"Beeswax candles" have a long-standing tradition of use in practical mysticism and ceremonial magick. Their application in ritual magick is often based on color, which correlates to an energy vibration projected and/or represented to assist the Sorcerer in achieving a correlated state to communicate with Reality. Prior to and during the operation—as with all tools of magick—the candles are "charged" with an intention or to represent a particular solid or object (target). While appearing in many operations, "candle magick" is its own nonspecific system that emphasizes exclusive use of candles as a catalyst for directing ritual energy. The "solid" represented by each candle—and the intention represented—is usually uttered out loud as it is lit to aid in focusing your attention and as a conscious affirmation.

Depending on experience and visualization abilities, "candle magick" may be simply performed through meditation and prayer—or as part of a more formalized method of spellcraft. As a means of sympathetic magick, "candle magick" requires imagination and creativity to be effective. Just as a Sorcerer creates a microcosm of the Universe when creating a *nemeton* —or casting a circle—so too does "candle magick" operate best when performed at an altar. This all represents a "chess-board" for the game of reality. By manipulating symbols on a representative playing field, you create a change first in your own consciousness, then project this into the reality at large.

If drawing something to you, use a candle to represent your-self and one (or more) for energies you want to attract. In this practice, candles are the "symbols" representing "solids." For several successive nights—usually three or seven—you will perform your working, each time moving the candle (that represents the external energy) closer to yours. The opposite may be performed as a reversal or banishing. Various colored candles may be used to represent specific concepts or energy streams. If a certain candle is representing you, it should be placed in the center of the altar or working area—as the Sor-cerer works this "game" out from the centralized perspective of *Self*. It remains fixed in the center always—other candles are arranged or moved around it. Some candle magick teach-ers suggest "astral colors" to represent individuals based on the zodiac. Words and names may also be written on them. Intentions and affirmations are spoken when they are lit.

| "Astral Colors"—(for Candle Magick) | |
|---|---|
| AQUARIUS – *Blue* | LEO – *Red* |
| PISCES – *White* | VIRGO – *Gold/Black* |
| ARIES – *White* | LIBRA – *Black* |
| TAURUS – *Red* | SCORPIO – *Brown* |
| GEMINI – *Red* | SAG. – *Gold/Black* |
| CANCER – *Green* | CAPRICORN – *Red* |

## CANDLE SPELLS & SORCERY

The following are basic examples of possible applications for candle magick. The Sorcerer is encouraged to develop their own ritual texts for these operations, as needed.

AFFAIRS—to break up the love affair of another: use astral colors to represent the people involved. Use a black candle for the breakup; a brown for the dying love; and a light green to cause jealousy and discord.

BAD HABITS—to overcome a bad habit: place a black candle in the middle representing the habit itself. Surround it with white candles (the opposite polar extreme of black) representing defeat of the habit itself.

DREAMS—to invoke prophetic dreams: surround your candle with a blue candle for peace and tranquility (a requirement dreaming). Use an orange candle to represent what you want to dream about and a white for sincerity and true vision.

FEAR—to overcome emotions of fear: surround your candle with several orange candles representing personal strength and self-confidence and a white candle for purity.

JEALOUSY—to arouse jealousy in another: surround their candle with a few brown candles of hesitation and uncertainty. Use light green candles to represent discord, illness and of course, jealousy.

MEDITATION—to aid acts of prayer or meditation: surround your candle with light blue candles of peace and tranquility.

POWER—to increase persuasion over other people: take both your candle and the candle of representing the subject on the altar. Each day, move their candle closer to yours, representing the magnetism. Surround your candle with purple for power and an orange candle demonstrating the attraction.

SPELLJAMMING—to remove a spell, hex, or curse: surround your candle with red for strength and vigor; and white for purity and sincerity. Have a black and brown candle on either side. Black symbolizes the cursed spell and brown represents the uncertainty of its castor. Move the black candle towards the brown (and away from yours) each day of the working to deflect their spell.

## MAGICKAL HERBALISM

If used properly, herbs may be potent ingredients for magick and spellcraft. Herbalism includes all use of dried herbs: incense, amulet bags (*satchets*), and oil manufacture. Herbs may be added to the altar, burned in a candle's flame (or as an incense), worn as oil (or perfume), and even placed in pouches to be hung, hidden or carried—as the case applies. The following are just a few examples of herbal energy associations:

> LUNAR – *Frankincense, Sandalwood*
> LOVE – *Rose, Cinnamon, Sandalwood, Patchouli*
> PEACE – *Bay/Laurel, Sandalwood*
> WEALTH – *Cloves, Nutmeg, Poppy seed, Cedar*
> STUDYING – *Cinnamon, Rosemary*
> SUCCESS – *Benzoin, Cinnamon, Dragon's Blood*
> PROTECTION – *Frankincense, Sandalwood, Rosemary*

Incense carries a long-standing tradition of use throughout the history of human spirituality and religion. It is often burned during magickal rituals and spells—but you may also wish to burn it in your house or environment after a working or spell to keep a specific energy current active or resonant—being sure not to dwell on the actual ritual, of course. You may also use scented oils or amulet bags to carry the personal effects of a spell with you as you go about your work-a-day life. The following are some popular herbal applications:

ALL-SPICE – *prosperity, relaxation*
APPLE – *love, happiness, relaxation*
CAMPHOR – *psychic power, letting go*
CINNAMON – *protection, sexual vigor*
EUCALYPTUS – *healing, purification*
JASMINE – *love, sleep, relaxation*
MUSK – *courage, sexual vigor*
MYRRH – *protection, purification, hex-breaking*
PATCHOULI – *peace of mind, sexual vigor*
ROSE – *love, peace, harmony, unity*
SANDALWOOD – *healing, protection*

"Amulet bags"—or *satchets*—are pouches, or you can make an appropriate bag using a four inch square swatch of cloth of appropriate color. Herbs and small items are placed in the center of the square and then the corners are brought together and tied up as a pouch. Alternately you could weave a draw-string around the outside of a cloth circle. According to popular lore: three, seven or nine herbs or items are added to a single bag, which is then *charged* during a related "spell."

PROTECTION—(*white*)—ash, basil, bay, dill, fennel, mistletoe, mugwort, periwinkle, rosemary, rowan, saint john's wort, trefoil, vervain.

HEALING—(*blue*)—garlic, eucalyptus, cinnamon, sage, saffron, sandalwood, lavender, rosemary, myrrh.

LOVE—(*red*)—apple, coriander, dragon's blood, jasmine, lavender, mandrake, marjoram, rose, rosemary, vervain, yarrow.

WEALTH / PROSPERITY—(*green*)—benzoin, cinnamon, patchouli, clove, sage, nutmeg, basil, dill.

## THE NORSE RUNES

Modern Sorcerers frequently use the "Norse-Elven" Futhark Runic Alphabet as a magickal substitution for English (Roman letters) when writing names and formulas in ritual. In addition to spellcraft, Norse-Elven runes also appear in esoteric lore for "key word divination" and "talisman" construction.

The word *"rune"* is of Germanic origin, meaning, "secret" or "hidden"—not altogether different than the Greek word, *"occult"* and Latin *"arcanum."* In other words, "runic magick" is a "secret magick," dealing with the "invisible" realm or Otherworld. This "Other" world is just as connected to the physical as *we* are, but its direct currents are best represented with symbols and glyphs. A similar practice of "runic magick" is found among the Celtic Druids using the "Ogham" Alphabet.* Both systems maintain a degree of affinity with "Nature."

Runic glyphs do, in fact, represent letters or "characters" of a written alphabet once native to Nordic languages. The same characters may be used to represent words and names in any language, just as a modern Sorcerer might also apply Ogham, Enochian characters or Cuneiform signs—each once a part of a native language, but also able to represent a common one. Mystical characters often substitute recognizable ones for magickal purposes including spellcraft, talisman construction and even personal notebooks or *"grimoires."*

When physically inscribing runes and glyphs—whether intentionally on talismans or some other more formal practice—it is important to treat the work as a magickal act. Then finally consecrate or "charge" the item officially in a spell-ritual. Sorcerers will trace a rune for its symbolic properties, using the action to generate personal vibrations of raised energy. All physical gestures and movements during "rune-casting" represent activity of a metaphysical energetic counterpart.

---

\* See also *"Elvenomicon: Secret Traditions of Elves and Faeries"* and/or *"Druid's Handbook: Ancient Magick for a New Age"* by Joshua Free.

"*Bind-runes*" are composite runes that *combine* more than one runic character to form a compound glyph or sign. It may be crafted based on the symbolic properties of the individual runes, or the letters of a name or word may be combined to form a representative "*sigil*"—thereby creating a more direct symbolic expression of a solid than even perhaps in a word.

| ᚠ | ᚢ | ᚦ | ᚨ | ᚱ | ᚲ | ᚷ | ᚹ | ᚺ | ᛁ | ᛃ |
|---|---|---|---|---|---|---|---|---|---|---|
| F | U | Th | A | R | C/K | G | W | H | N | I | J |

| ᛗ | ᚲ | ᛉ | ᛋ | ᛏ | ᛒ | ᛖ | ᛗ | ᛚ | ᛜ | ᛞ | ᛟ |
|---|---|---|---|---|---|---|---|---|---|---|---|
| Y | P | X/Z | S | T | B | E | M | L | Ing | D | O |

FEHU—"F"—*prosperity, possessions, wealth, power.*
URUZ—"U"—*strength, manifestation, sacrifice.*
THURISA—"Th"—*destruction, defense, gateway, demons.*
ANSUZ—"A"—*signal, expression, reception, transformation.*
RAIDO—"R"—*right action, wagon, journey.*
KANO—"C"/"K"—*opening, creativity, torch.*
GEBO—"G"—*partnership, sacrifice, magick, sexuality.*
WUNJO—"W"—*joy, harmony, fellowship.*
HAGALZ—"H"—*disruption, hail, framework.*
NAUTHIZ—"N"—*constraint, deliverance, persistence.*
ISA—"I"—*ice, concentration, standstill.*
JERA—"J"—*harvest, fertility, peace.*
EIHWAZ—"Y"—*defense, yew tree, life and death cycles.*
PERTH—"P"—*initiation, karma, assertiveness.*
ALGIZ—"X"/"Z"—*protection, life, the Elf.*
SOWELU—"S"—*wholeness, sun, victory.*
TEIWAZ—"T"—*warrior, justice, god's judgment.*
BERKANA—"B"—*birth, life cycle, growth, birch tree.*
EHWAZ—"E"—*movement, the horse, soul travel.*
MANNAZ—"M"—*humans, intelligence, the self.*

LAGUZ—"L"—*flow, lake life, fertility.*
INGUZ—"Ng"—*fertility, power, potential, raw energy.*
DAGAZ—"D"—*day light, breakthroughs, prosperity.*
OTHILA—"O"—*property, prosperity, separations.*

## PUTTING IT ALL TOGETHER

Why are so many people drawn to spellcraft and ritual magick? Likely it is because of the promises of material gain and potential powers offered. . . And the Sorcerer is no exception, for there is obvious merit to applying low magickal spellcraft to more effectively shape the universe around us.

I warn those who practice the arts not to become obsessive or give in to the "hunger" of mundane power alone. There are much deeper levels of "magick"—of which *ritualization* is but the first rung on the *Ladder of Ascension*. Don't allow "low magick" to rule your life—for it is only in our *naivete* that we believe ourselves masters when we still carry the craving.

Be smart! If you have an SAT test—*study!* If you have a job interview—*look your best!* You can always use spellcraft to assist your life, but don't expect it to take the responsibility. It is *you* that possesses the ability to respond. Some Sorcerers believe "ritual magick" should be used solely as a last resort. I have met others that believe you only "get so much" in a single lifetime, or that certain magick will somehow age the body prematurely—while the other half believes that it will help to keep them young perpetually. We can thank movies and medias for propagating some of these stereotypes—but in the end, it really just comes down to using some plain old "wizards-sense."

# ELEMENTAL MAGICK & DRUID POWER

As we perceive them in the fragmented physical world, there appear to be four primary elements of "Nature"—plus a fifth of "*quintessence,*" sometimes called "*Akasha.*"

---

EARTH provides structure, substance and foundation.
    They are the keys to *abundance.*

AIR offers communication, illumination, focus and clarity.
    They are the keys of *intellect.*

FIRE gives strength, courage, vitality and faith.
    They are the keys to *protection.*

WATER brings transformation, healing and purity.
    They are the keys of *inner peace.*

---

## ELEMENTAL MAGICK—"ELEMENTALISM"

Magickal lore of the "Elements"—sometimes called *Elementalism—is* found at the heart of most modern "magical" revivals of esoteric mysticism, particularly Earth-oriented systems rooted in "Nature." But, this elemental model of understanding is universal throughout the cosmos. We simply learn it by applying the paradigm to the level of reality we can see and touch in the world—which we are immediately immersed in. But, all of these forces are interconnected, forming the basis of energetic relationships and interactions taking place at all levels of existence simultaneously in the cosmos.

Ancient Druids integrated elemental qualities of the elements into "mystical" and "magical" paradigms—yet this fundamental knowledge is no more "supernatural" than laws and tables of elements in "Chemistry"—so named for its origins in the "dark arts." This understanding of Nature provides us our storehouse of physical and metaphysical knowledge—a basis to build our interactive understanding of "how things work" and "what we can do" to cause desired results. This alchemical combination of forces and elements is the same that fuels creation—the same processes and Cosmic Laws that are in effect with or without our belief and participation. Druids use an understanding of energetic variables—as they relate to the "Four Elements"—to conduct "magickal work" that promotes personal change and ascent on the Ladder of Ascension.

The universe is a "singularity"—there is no separation. Yet, in our manifest world of infinite parts, we can find an infinite number of connections. We can begin with a twofold dualism, working our way through a threefold triad or a fourfold quadrology. . . In fact, for as many ways as we can divide wholeness, we can find a way to make the paradigm work. The mind is amazing in its ability to separate, fix labels and categorize a myriad of parts—inventing more knowledge to *know*. For our purposes—ancient non-chemical paradigms involving "Elementalism" relay the model best as a four-fold division of basic elements: *Earth, Air, Fire* and *Water*.

A basic four-fold elemental model is preferred by most practitioners, regardless of the tradition involved. It is popular in the Western Magical Tradition because it follows natural symmetry and cycles we easily identify in Nature; it easily pairs with the "four corners" of the World—meaning four cardinal directions—and likewise the corners, sides or quadrangles of a ceremonial temple or ritual circle. Material elements—*earth* and *air*—divide the basic essence of creation into solids and gases. Later "scientific" classifications determined liquid—or *water*—to be a composite of various additional elements, and *fire* was eventually rejected from the elemental model as a "combustion process" or transformation, but not an elemental component in itself. And—that is what conventional scientific vocabulary semantics have to say about it.

In the current author's personal model,[*] *earth* and *air* correspond to the first two (primary) forms of manifestation that modern science is familiar with: gravity ($G$) and electromagnetism ($EM$). Discovery of the other two subatomic nuclear forces completes the fourfold "standard model" of Western Elementalism. In this system, *fire* corresponds to the weak nuclear ($W$) force responsible for radiation, fusion and heat. The qualities from the *water* element best correspond to the strong nuclear ($S$) force that bonds and unites particles together all across the fabric of space or *Sea of Infinity*.

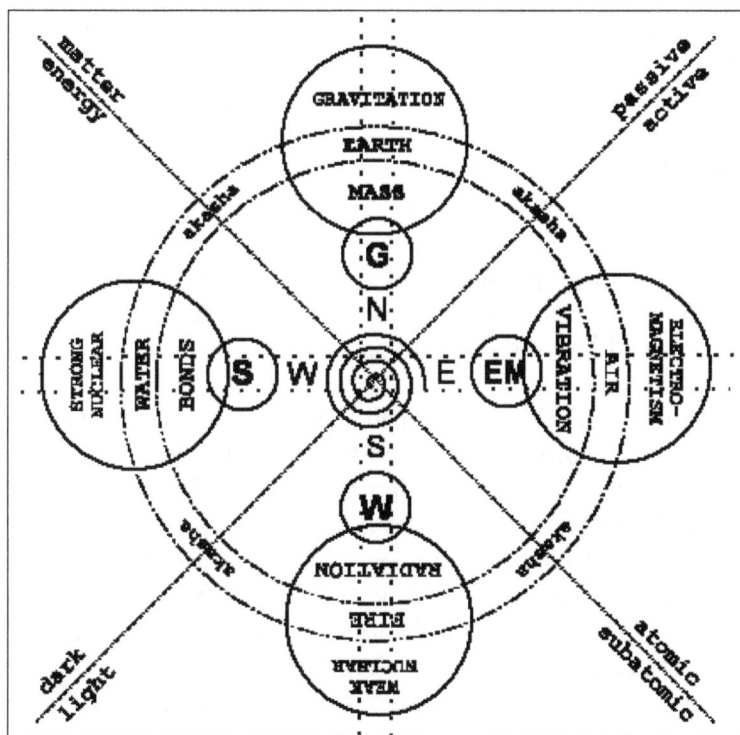

---

[*]   First outlined in the 2008 edition of *"Arcanum: The Great Magical Arcanum"* by Joshua Free.

"Elementalism"—its study and implementation—is an integral part of the "Druid Path." In order to fully appreciate the symphony of energies at play in the Universe, the seeker must also learn to perceive the elemental forces as something more than just the "perceptibly physical" manifestations and forms most easily beheld. For example—*Earth* is more than ground and rocks; *Fire* is more than a candle-flame; *Air* is more than just wind—and so forth.

Metaphysical and esoteric lore refers to the most perfect or pure manifestations of these elemental forces as "Elemental Kingdoms," existing outside the material range that humans are aware of. These concentrations of elemental energy interact with our world—the condensed physical level—but radiate from a "higher" encompassing dimension, with its *Rays* interconnected with all aspects of our visible world.

Where some authors and traditions relay elemental lore as an introductory side-note—or as simply a foundation for some other execution of practical or "ritual magick," as we have presented in previous chapter-lessons—Druids spent a considerable amount of their lifetime working and meditating in Nature, ultimately leading to a systematized understanding of elemental energies and their interconnectivity related to all aspects of life and existence.

According to Druidic Lore—the "Doctrine of Authority"—the greater the amount of time spent having a communication of energy with a specific "Elemental Kingdom," the greater the state of "mastery" or "authority" achieved with that particular element. An integration of practical knowledge and the experience of energetic work with each of these elements becomes a matter of personal individuality—the point where a Druidic curriculum must be shaped for an initiate—but ultimately working through each of the elements, one by one.[*]

---

[*] See also *"The Druid's Handbook: Ancient Magick for a New Age"* by Joshua Free.

## ELEMENTAL SIGNS OF PORTAL

Druids perceived that basic geometric symbols are tied to the elements. They may be traced in the air with an appropriate tool—or power finger—and envisioned in an appropriate elemental color to invite an energetic presence of the Elemental Kingdoms to your ritual, environment or *nemeton*. They may also be used as glyphs or *Keys* in other magickal applications, such as "Elemental Tablets" to set at each direction in ritual.

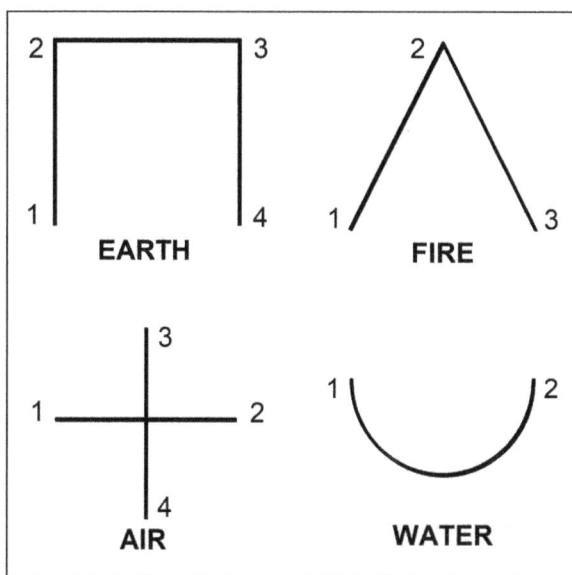

## ELEMENTAL BEINGS—"ELEMENTALS"

Sorcerers believe in the conscious or intelligent energies that possess characteristics based on the "element" they are created from. The term "elemental" may also relate to anything pertaining to the elements themselves or the philosophy and practice of "elemental magick." Sentient beings exist in elemental domains or kingdoms wrapped in unseen dimensions. They also possess practical faculties—including the ability to travel (or transition) between "dimensions."

According to "Edaphic" (Elven Druid) Tradition, Elementals may even have the ability to mate with humans when assuming material form—something that *has* happened, causing the creation of the faerie folk that were driven underground with the rise of human populations during the Dark Ages.* Elemental blood still exists in some recesses of the genetic pool. These metaphysical beings also have the ability to "walk-in" to an existing material body—or simulacrum—through a process called *"transignation."*

Elementals appear in global mythologies, now perceived as "creatures of fantasy." The attitude taken by most New Age practitioners is that these beings are not "imaginary" in the sense of being fictitious, but their energetic memory is, for the most, confined to the Astral Plane or "Otherworld." Given the interconnectedness (unification) of all elements, physical and spiritual dimensions, these conscious currents of energy may be easily reached from the Body of Light and/or *nemeton*. In ceremonial and ritual magick, Elemental beings are often summoned to directly lend energy to magickal workings.

Inter-dimensional and elemental beings are some of the most difficult aspects of magick to conceive of from the Human perspective of traditional (conditioned) thought. The simple explanation is that elementals encountered in rituals are a projection from the Sorcerer's consciousness made tangible by thousands of years of energetic concentration and condensation on planet Earth. The resonant archetypal memory remains and may continue to be fed more energy over time, provided that traditions continue to be observed. Grimoires such as the *Keys of Solomon*, depict a different picture. According to these medieval sorcerers, intelligences are emanated or given substance to by a natural elemental phenomenon existent in the Universe. Whether clouds, fire or the rays of the Sun, the wizards and mystics of the ages have perceived the energy as both intelligent and dynamic—not merely static.

---

\* See also *"Elvenomicon -or- Secret Traditions of Elves and Faeries"* by Joshua Free.

The pantheistic view of the Universe has led most uninitiated to misinterpret the metaphysical philosophy of elemental thresholds and portal phenomenon. The rain, in and of itself, is not considered intelligent or alive—what the rain provides is an elemental "charge," energetically polarized to generate a higher affinity to a particular energy type within the affected space. This threshold phenomenon may cause the area to resonate with specific spiritual intelligences, which then are simply called "rain-spirits" in indigenous shamanic lore.

## BASIC TREE ENERGY-WORK

Druids were well learned in tapping into the energy of trees for rituals, magick, spiritual practices and communication. Using "Ogham" and other tree lore, the Sorcerer might also wish to tap into energies of certain tree-types based on their metaphysical attributes (correspondences). Basic tree energy work may be performed to aid in restoring personal vitality, to increase endurance and/or commune with Nature.

---

### _Absorbing Tree Energy_

• Go to a special tree (beginners should use a pine tree);
• Touch your fingers to the sharp needle ends;
• Hold for at least three minutes;
• Visualize a greenish-white stream of energy flowing from the tree to you.

---

## BASIC TREE COMMUNICATION

The Druids acknowledged that all life possessed a spiritual energy within it—connected to the Source of All. Concerning trees—Druids recognized them as tremendous storehouses of Nature's power and even as living libraries of earth memory. The following approach is a simple, but time-proven, method.

---

### *Basic Tree Communication*

• Go to a special or sacred tree;
• Sit close, legs crossed, palms spread, touching the tree;
• Begin meditative breathing;
• Progressively relax the whole body;
• Speak clearly to the tree from your I-AM-Self:

> *Spirit of the sacred tree*
> *Make yourself known to me*
> *I invoke you for the sake of speech*
> *And wish to learn all you will teach.*

• Feel the physical sensation of the bark of the tree;
• Visualize green life-force energy leaving your hands;
• See white energy coming back and forming a cloud of energy above your head.

---

When the tree is ready it will project imagery into the cloud formed above your head. Trees communicate using graphics and beginners may even only see colored bands. With practice you will be able to understand the imagery received and project image responses into the cloud.

## ELEMENTAL RITUAL

This solitary ritual is based on lore from the Druid Tradition. Prepare a ritual *nemeton* outdoors using your own height as the diameter—perhaps arranging a stone circle perimeter. Be sure to bring your "Elemental Tools" with you and set them out at the proper quarters of the magick circle.

Go to the center of the nemeton and say:

> *I stand on a threshold between worlds at a time that is not a time, in a place that is not a place, on a day that is not a day, between the worlds and beyond, yet I am here. I who occupy this sacred center is at one with many gods who are but faces*

*of the One God. I claim as birthright, for this moment outside of time, to assume the Godform of my true Self.*

In the north, take a pinch of sea-salt, and sprinkle some onto your tongue. Take another pinch and sprinkle it onto the ground. Trace the Earth Sign of Portal with the stone and say:

*I invoke you O powers of the Earth, the kingdom of Stone. I call out to the kingdom of Falias, Ghobas and Morfessas. Hear my call. Hear my call. I summon your infinite powers. Come forth from the North. By this sign you shall be known.*

Go to the east and take a handful of petals (from a rose) to scatter in the air—and let them float to the ground. Using the air tool, trace the Air Sign of Portal and say:

*I invoke you O powers of the Air, the kingdom of Wind. I call out to the kingdom of Esras, Gorias and Paraldas. Hear my call. Hear my call. I summon your infinite powers. Come forth from the East. By this sign you you shall be known.*

At the south, burn a Druidic incense mixture of mistletoe and oak. Trace the Fire Sign of Portal with a ritual blade, saying:

*I invoke you O powers of Fire, the kingdom of Flame. I call out to the kingdom of the Flames of Consciousness, the kingdom of Finias, Uscias and Djinas. Hear my call. Hear my call. I summon your infinite powers. Come forth from the South. By this sign you shall be known.*

Go to the west, drink some (water) from your cup, Then pour some out and trace the Water Sign of Portal, saying:

*I invoke you O powers of Water, the kingdom of the Sea, I call out to the kingdom of the Waves of the Subconsciousness, the kingdom of Murias, Semias and Niksas. Hear my call. Hear my call. I summon your infinite powers. Come forth now from the West. By this sign you shall be known.*

Return to the center of the circle and say:

> *Elemental spirits of the outer realms—bless, guard and shield*
> *me always. Around me and within me, above and below me.*
> *Protect me from myself and others. I declare by the strength of*
> *the Elder Gods, the Great Ideals of the mysteries and the lofti-*
> *est heights of the Guardians of the Universe.*

The elemental ritual is completed. If desired, other magickal workings and rites may also be performed within this consecrated/sacred space. From a Druid or "Elementalist" standard, this rite reflects a superior method of "casting a circle" for Nature magick. Written ritual texts such as these will generally only provide instructions for the "actions" taking place, leaving an initiate dependent on their previous experience regarding "ritual magick" fundamentals and "energy work" to transform allegorical scripts into potential power.

# THE GOLDEN DAWN OF MODERN SORCERERS

Perhaps the most publicly famous and influential magickal "secret society" or "Order"—at the dawn of the 20th Century —the *Hermetic Order of the Golden Dawn*" was founded in 1895, a combined effort developed by *Rosicrucians* and *Freemasons*. It attracted membership of very prestigious mystical writers, including: W.B. Yeats, Arthur Edward Waite, Israel Regardie, Dion Fortune and yes, even Aleister Crowley.

Structure of G.D. (*Golden Dawn*) systems of "apprenticeship" (degrees) consists of 10+1 "grades" of initiation and study derived from the Hebrew *Kabbalah:*—

| THE GOLDEN DAWN SYSTEM OF INITIATION |
|---|
| 0-0: <u>Neophyte</u> |
| 1-10: <u>Zelator</u>—(*Malkuth*/earth) |
| 2-9: <u>Theoricus</u>—(*Yesod*/air) |
| 3-8: <u>Practicus</u>—(*Hod*/water) |
| 4-7: <u>Philsophus</u>—(*Netzach*/fire) |
| 5-6: <u>Adeptus Minor</u>—(*Tiphareth*/harmony) |
| 6-5: <u>Adeptus Major</u>—(*Geburah*/might) |
| 7-4: <u>Adeptus Exemptus</u>—(*Chesed*/mercy) |
| 8-3: <u>Magister Templi</u>—(*Binah*/understanding) |
| 9-2: <u>Magus</u>—(*Chokmah*/wisdom) |
| 10-1: <u>Ipsissimis</u>—(*Kether*/Akasha) |

Samuel Mathers—better known as S.L. MacGregor Mathers— together with William Wynn Westcott and W.R. Woodman—

both *Rosicrucians*—formed the original *"Hermetic Order of the Golden Dawn."* After Westcott brought an obscure manuscript to *Mathers* to translate, they discovered rituals of an already extinct *germanic secret society* called the "Golden Dawn" (possibly even *"Aurum Solis"*).

## S.L. MACGREGOR MATHERS

When Westcott approached him, *Mathers* was already busy translating coveted magical "grimoires" into English—among these the *Keys of Solomon, Goetia* and *Sacred Book of Magic of Abramelin the Mage.* He contributed considerably to the publicly available lore of practical *Kabbalah,* and suggested a secret ceremonial chamber "vault" for GD rituals be modeled after the tomb of *Christian Rosenkreutz*—a seven-sided room, each wall being five feet wide by eight feet tall. Higher degrees of the GD focused on the *Kabbalah* and Enochian Magick embedded within obscure manuscripts and grimoires. The emphasis on mysticism and practical magick attracted many "would-be wizards" to approach the Great Work from exclusively ceremonial paradigms rather than the more philosophical. This later culminated into the *"Golden Dawn System of Magic."*

## THE SECRET COUNCIL

In addition to developing a standard practice of "ceremonial magic" mixed with *Kabbalistic* lore and a revived interest in magical grimoires, the highest GD degrees focused on *Enochian Magic*, which emphasized communication with Otherworld intelligences—often presented in the guise of "angels." The loftiest pursuits of the Order clearly targeted practices that would promote inter-dimensional contact. In fact, Mathers referred to a *"Third Circle"* or *"Third Order"*—beyond the Outer and Inner Circles/Orders of the GD organization—composed of "Ascended Masters" or "Invisible Chiefs," entities that were consulted with by GD "Second Circle" members.

## ALEISTER CROWLEY

Although perhaps the most famous member of the original Order, Aleister Crowley never was allowed initiation to the GD Inner Circle. This was possibly wise, since Crowley later published the GD "Outer Court" tradition to the uninitiated. When Mathers refused to "see him through" to the higher degrees, Crowley retaliated against him and GD with magickal warfare. This sparked so much public attention that both members were eventually unseated from GD, and W.B. Yeats maintained leadership in Mathers absence.

## ISRAEL REGARDIE

After Crowley published his own version of the GD materials, Israel Regardie felt obligated to clarify the effort, republishing all original GD materials in four volumes, titled simply *The Golden Dawn.* He later compiled a more accessible version called *The Complete System of Golden Dawn Magic.* While the organization is now a feint shadow of what it once was, many modern Magicians and Sorcerers attempt to revive the GD structure and system, or else self-initiate themselves into its practices. The richness and symbolism of the ceremonies, strongly reminiscent of Freemasonry, are often considered outdated by many modern practitioners in the New Age. The sheer bulk and *crypticism* of GD literature is enough to turn novices away, not to mention its numerous occult errors— but the GD methodology still holds many valid contributions.

## ARTHUR EDWARD WAITE

In 1903, William Butler Yeats—yes, the famed poet— replaced S.L. MacGregor Mathers as the head of the GD Order, causing a schism among existing membership. One of the most prestigious GD members at that time—and an initiate of the "Inner Order" or "Second Order"—was Arthur Edward (A.E.) Waite.

Deciding that the new direction of GD leadership was turning the group toward more philosophical and "poetic" ideals, as opposed to stronger mystical and esoteric pursuits, Waite left to form his own branch of the "Second Order"—retaining the "magical system" of its Rosicrucian and other esoteric roots— and calling his secret society the "Ordo Rosae Rubae et Aureae Crucis" (R.R. et A.C.)--"The Order of the Ruby Red Rose and Golden Cross." As such, A.E. Waite rewrote many of the original GD rites of initiation and other standards of operation for his new Order.

Previously, in 1898, A.E. Waite released *The Book of Black Magic and Pacts*—later reprinted as *The Complete Grimoire* and *The Complete Book of Ceremonial Magic*. The book extracts critical excerpts and rituals from many now-popular *grimoires*. Although quite critical of the techniques—actually alluding that literal exploration into these futile notebooks was a pit-trap —Waite's presentation brought many obscure manuscripts to light, those formerly only known to, and accessed by, GD initiates. As a result, Waite is considered a significant influence toward the increased appearance of "ceremonial magic" in "mainstream occultism" throughout the 20th century. But, it is perhaps not for *this* effort that he is *best* known. . .

## THE GOLDEN DAWN OF "TAROT"

The most famous public contribution of Arthur Edward Waite is the "Rider-Waite Tarot" deck. It remains one of the most recognizable worldwide graphic versions of tarot symbolism. Its corresponding book, *The Pictorial Key to the Tarot*, released in 1910, correlates traditional tarot symbolism with alchemical, GD and kabbalistic lore—and remains the most widely circulated interpretation for meditation and "*divination.*"

Lore suggests that the modern French word "tarot" is derived from "tarocchi," an Italian plural form of "tarocco" meaning "trump." The twenty-two cardinal archetypes of the "Major

Arcana" are often referred to as "trumps" or "trump cards." The word "tarotee" describes the cross-hatch line pattern that graced the card-backs of most early decks. The "Minor Arcana" is the precursor to the modern "playing card" decks, which may also be used as an "oracle system."

The Major Arcana of primary archetypes are esoterically superior to the remainder of the deck and may be effectively studied and used for meditation and divination independent of the others. The "Pathway" demonstrated in their symbolism is frequently applied to our knowledge of, for example: Jungian archetypes; the stages of alchemical transformation; the journey of the *Self* or spirit toward wholeness—via the Right Way or Ladder of Ascension.

Regardless of whether or not ancient Egyptians and Hermetic Magicians actively used a "tarot card" system—as often alluded in related guides—the GD and its members researched and wrote hundreds of pages providing interpretations and ritual correspondences. In addition to "Gypsy Divination," as they call it, the GD uses the Major Arcana for "pathworking" —focusing/meditating on symbolism of a card to trigger certain mental responses and astral visions. Some operations suggest meditating on a key card before going to sleep and then placing it under your pillow to inspire a lucid-dream.

The Major Arcana will be the focus of our current discourse— those cards are numbered "0" to "21" (sometimes in Roman numerals) and carry key title-names. These are easily separable from the rest of the pack—which is referred to as the "Minor Arcana." These other cards represent the ten stations or "*sephiroth*" of the Hebrew *Kabbalah* as divided by four elemental "suits."

"Keys" for the Major Arcana are described below. These may be used for any application—but they should be studied prior to practical use—either in "ceremonial magic," meditation, or oracular divination—to ensure coherent familiarity.

# THE TAROT—"MAJOR ARCANA"

0—FOOL: Crown of Wisdom; the arts of divination; and the "Primary Universal Motion" acting through the air element on the zodiac.
-Keywords: crossroads, decisions, new beginnings and taking measure before acting.

1—MAGICIAN: Crown of Understanding; the arts of healing; and the "Prima Materia" acting through (philosophic) Mercury onto Saturn.
-Keywords: application of willpower and ability, learning and use of knowledge.

2—HIGH PRIESTESS: Crown of Beauty; the abilities of clairvoyance (spirit vision); and the "Primum Mobile" acting though the Moon onto the Sun.
-Keywords: inspiration, intuition, spiritual connection and uncovering hidden influences.

3—EMPRESS: Wisdom of Understanding; the arts and experience of love; and the Sphere of the Zodiac acting through Venus on Saturn.
-Keywords: fertility, growth, joy, prosperity and satisfaction.

4—EMPEROR: Wisdom of Beauty; acts of consecration; and the Sphere of the Zodiac acting through Aries on the Sun (beginning of the spring season).
-Keywords: exterior authority, inner balance, responsibility and use of experience.

5—HIGH PRIEST (HIEROPHANT): Wisdom of Mercy; ability to summon inner strength; and the Sphere of the Zodiac acting through Taurus on Jupiter.
-Keywords: open-mindedness or stubbornness (reversed), recognition of truth and solidifying foundations.

6—LOVERS: Understanding of Beauty; the gift of prophecy; and Saturn acting through Gemini on the Sun.
-Keywords: changes, determination, possible indication of relationship and love.

7—CHARIOT: Understanding of Strength (Severity); the magick of enchantment; and Saturn acting through Cancer onto Mars.
-Keywords: application of energy, movement, self-discipline, travel, triumph and success in a cycle.

8—STRENGTH: Mercy of Strength (Severity); the ability to temper the wild nature of animals or men; and Jupiter acting through Leo onto Mars.
-Keywords: disillusionment, need for organization, use of personal strength and assurance of success if temperance is exercised.

9—HERMIT: Mercy of Beauty; the arts of invisibility; and Jupiter acting through Virgo on the Sun.
-Keywords: experimentation, guidance, responsibility, true wisdom and withdrawal.

10—WHEEL OF FORTUNE: Mercy of Victory; the Right Way; and Jupiter acting directly onto Venus.
-Keywords: chance, cycles, opportunity, randomness and the ups and downs of life.

11—JUSTICE: Strength (Severity) of Beauty; guiding justice; and Mars acting through the Scale of Libra on the Sun.
-Keywords: consideration of all factors, equality, fairness and possible external influences.

12—HANGED MAN: Strength (Severity) of Glory/ Splendor; the use of talismans; and Mars acting through the water element onto Mercury.
-Keywords: changing directions, the need for foresight, indecision, transitions ("mid-life crisis") and self-sacrifice.

13—DEATH: Beauty of Victory; the arts of necromancy; and the Sun acting through Scorpio on Venus.
-Keywords: abrupt change, letting go, transition and unfortunate realizations.

14—TEMPERANCE (BALANCE): Beauty of Foundation; alchemy or transmutation; and the Sun acting through Sagittarius on the Moon.
-Keywords: execute balance, seek security and harmony, slow down and temper your emotions.

15—DEVIL (HORNED ONE): Beauty of Glory (False Splendor); the use of the evil eye; and the Sun acting through Capricorn onto Mercury.
-Keywords: arrogance, bondage, egotism, pride, materialism and the need for self-control.

16—TOWER (FALLING TOWER): Victory of Glory (Splendor); the use of curses for revenge; and Venus acting through Mars upon Mercury.
-Keywords: breakdown, clinging to the old, false hopes and sudden changes.

17—STARS: Victory of the Foundation (Fundamental World); the use of true astrology; and Venus acting through Aquarius on the Moon.
-Keywords: future accomplishments, high hopes, ideals, and the need for clarity and spiritual aid.

18—MOON: Victory of the Kingdom (Material World); elemental magick and faerie glamourie; and Venus acting through Pisces onto *a priori* elemental forces.
-Keywords: dreams, hidden influences/forces, intuition needed, self-reliance required and subtle changes to come.

19—SUN: Glory (Splendor) of the Kingdom (Material World); the use of grimoires or evocation; and Mercury acting through the Sun onto the Moon.

-Keywords: blessings, brightness, brilliance, fulfillment, happiness, honesty, joy and laughter.

20—JUDGMENT: Glory (Splendor) of the Foundation (Spiritual Realm); wealth magick; and Mercury acting through Fire (or Akasha) on cosmic elements.
-Keywords: completion near, forthcoming renewal, guidance needed, looking ahead and an observation period.

21—UNIVERSE (WORLD): The Foundation (Fundamental Level) of the Kingdom (Material World); Earth-oriented magick; and the Cosmos.
-Keywords: cycle ends, freedom, perfection, satisfaction, success and triumph.

When performing oracular divination, the tarot deck is cut and shuffled by the operator. Cards are occasionally allowed to fall—this usually happens anyways—which are then put back into the deck "reversed," so that some cards may be placed upside-down in a spread—with the figures standing on their heads. These cards are interpreted as the antithesis of the keywords described above, or else indicative of an extreme need for attention or to acquire such attributes. Some practitioners simply cut the deck, reverse half of the cards, and then continue shuffling. Others believe that no intentional reversal of cards should ever be attempted and that cards reversed from previous readings should remain in the pack this way. As with everything else given in this book—use your own intuition and experiment freely.

The most common tarot card "*spread*" or "layout" is known as the ten-card Celtic or Gypsy method. It was also taught in the Golden Dawn System. This formula requires placing ten randomly drawn cards in a predetermined pattern or *spread*. The seer or "reader" posses the question and begins drawing each card, one by one, while reading or stating the function of each card position. At the end, all of the cards are interpreted individually and then in relation to one another.

## THE TAROT—"CELTIC CROSS SPREAD"

1. "This envelops you."—The *significator* card; the observer of the question, the general atmosphere of the *querent*, aura or personal influence surrounding the person in question.

2. "This blocks you."—The card representing forces of opposition acting against the particular situation. This is the primary barrier or obstacle to a successful outcome.

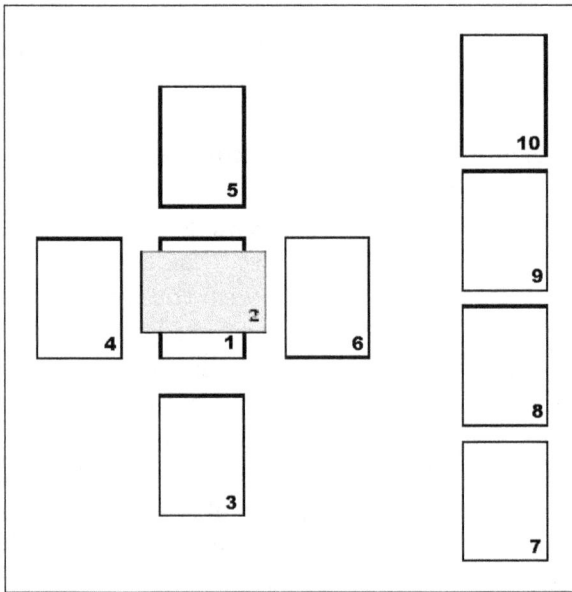

3. "This is beneath you."—The card representing the basic foundation of the situation, or that which is already strongly evident or may be drawn from as a resource.

4. "This is behind you."—The card representing past influences or forces influencing the situation that have already passed, including experience that may be drawn from as a resource.

5. "This crowns you."—The card representing the most evident overt ideals, goals or aims of the situation; perhaps also the motives or light shining on the work, but the energies that you are or should be drawing "down."

6. "This is before you."—The card representing the direct action forthcoming and the near-future influences that may be expected or drawn from as a resource.

7. "This is your true persona."—This card reflects how you should present yourself to others involved, or else carry yourself to bring about the given situation.

8. "This is your house."—This card depicts how others pertaining to the situation perceive you. This card also reflects your social self, meaning the external influence that others (and your environment) project onto you and the situation.

9. "This is your hopes and fears."—This card reflects symbolism of that will ultimately become evident on the current course of actions, but first requires right thinking and right action to carry through.

10. "This is the final result."—This card provides a predicted ultimate outcome of the situation (based on the current movement of energy, forces and influences). The oracular reading only displays the most probable movement of energy, but it may also assist in directing the reader's attention to other key cards that display what is needed to either change a given result or ensure a successful outcome.

# HIGH MAGICK OF THE GOLDEN DAWN

One of the most frequently used preliminary ritual workings from the Golden Dawn System of Magic is called the *Lesser Banishing Ritual of the Pentagram*, which in itself is composed of several popular high magickal rites, including the *Kabbalistic Cross* and *Middle Pillar Rite.* It is most clearly—and indisputably—derived from a famous ancient Mesopotamian rite, called the *"Incantation of Eridu"*—the same rite integrated into every ancient Babylonian ritual!

Magical "gestures" corresponding to the *Kabbalistic* version of the rite are also the origin for a practice of "self-blessing" commonly called the *"sign of the cross."* Note: the order that the shoulders are touched is reversed from the traditionally used *"sign of the cross,"* which is a banishing or warding act, meant to "keep something away." The *Kabbalistic Cross* method is "active" and "invoking"—inviting energies in. The incantation is actually a part of the *Lord's Prayer* given by Jesus: "The Kingdom, the power and the glory, forever. Amen."

---

### The Kabbalistic Cross Rite

• Stand in the east and imagine yourself becoming very tall, with your head in the clouds and your feet firmly on the surface of the Earth.

• Intone *"Ah-toh"* using your right (projective) index finger to touch the middle of your forehead as you imagine the white ray of light descending upon you from the Supreme Sphere (*Sephiroth*) of *Kether* from the Kabbalah.

• Intone "*Mahl-kuth*" (*Malkuth*) as you touch the middle of your chest, feeling light descending from your head to that spot, establishing the main vertical shaft of the Kabbalistic Cross.

• Intone "*Veh-geh-du-lah,*" touching your left shoulder, and feeling the Divine ray of light appear and grow.

• Carry your hand to the right shoulder as you intone "*Veh-geh-bu-rah*" feeling the arm or horizontal bar of the cross blazing before you.

• Clasp your hands at your chest and meditate upon the Cross of Clear Light, speaking "*Ah-mehn.*"

In its modern form—as practiced today—the *Middle Pillar Rite* resembles early *masonic* or *Templar* rituals, using passwords and imagery mentioned in ancient initiations of some unknown esoteric sect near Jerusalem. The names of the two polarized pillars—either represented in a physical temple or simply imagined for the rite—are "*Boaz*" and "*Jachin,*" names of the pillars (from *Masonic* lore) at the entrance threshold of King Solomon's Temple. The pillars represent energetic duality manifest in physical existence in the form of light and dark, male and female, &tc. When facing east, the pillar on the left (north) is the Black Pillar (*Boaz*) of Severity. On the right (south) is the White Pillar (*Jachim*) of Mercy. If you are facing west—as some versions of the rite instruct—then the Black Pillar is on the right and the White Pillar is on the left.

During meditation, a practitioner imagines themselves as the crystalline pillar—a harmonic balance between two extremes. Some contemporary *magicians* use the "*Middle Pillar Rite*" as a means of activating—or achieving active awareness of—the

"Body of Light" or "Light-Body," a personal mystic state that must be achieved in order to successfully conduct "high magickal" work.

---

### *The Middle Pillar Rite*

• Stand in the west, close your eyes, visualize the pillars on either side of you and meditate on their significance. Reflect/radiate the powers of each pillar and feel yourself balancing the opposing forces within you.

• Take a deep breath and raise your awareness to above your head; feel a divine ray of light form in this energy center (or *crown chakra*) and intone: "*Eh-heh-eh.*"

• Feel the light descend to the base of your neck (*throat chakra*) and intone: "*Yod-Heh-Vahv-Heh Ehl-oh-heem.*"

• Feel the light descending down your back to the base of your spine and intone: "*Shah-dye El Chye.*"

• Then feel the light move through your pelvic region as you intone: "*Ah-doh-nye Hah-ah-retz.*"

• Finally, the light moved to your feet (*root chakra*) and intone: "*Mahl-kooth.*"

• Many GD practitioners will supplement this rite with the Kabbalistic Cross Rite previously described.

---

The "*Lesser Banishing Ritual of the Pentagram*"—or "LBRP"—is found in opening and closing procedures of all operations of the GD *System* of magic. As either a preliminary banishing or a finalizing one, the rite is conducted to "clear," "banish" or "neutralize" existing energies of a space used to conduct magic—any space treated as "sacred" or consecrated or as a temporary imitation of the ancient 'temple-shrines' of the *gods*. In modern "ritual magick" the LBRP is used to "cast a circle" or "consecrate" a space with the intention of doing magic—cleansing the air of any preexisting or negative energies at the beginning, as well as any resonant (or residual) energy remaining at the end of the working. While it is true that any area may become "charged" or else "enchanted" with repeated magical use, all "active energies" must be directed accordingly during a ritual—not allowed to linger. This is resolved in most standard practices.

The *pentagram* "traced" by the Sorcerer in the air for the LBRP operation is always "banishing"—which is a description of the "way" or "direction" that energy is traced for the star-pattern; essentially meaning where the starting point is and in what direction the lines trace the shape.

There are differing opinions—or traditions—in modern practice concerning "colors" of energy envisioned when tracing *pentagrams* for the LBRP. Some of the older (original) methods describe a white or silvery band of light, yet some other contemporary traditions—mainly those inspired by *Donald Michael Kraig*—have advocated use of the *blue ray*, possibly due to its protective qualities in some evocation rites.

The *pentagram* may be traced with a "magical implement"—such as a wand or dagger-blade—or it can be traced simply with the practitioners right (or projective) index finger. The challenge here is maintaining the visualization and energetic awareness of the *pentagrams* as the Sorcerer moves around the circle—and throughout the ritual work. When the center of a *pentagram* is pointed to, the Sorcerer should "feel" and "see" the *pentagram* as "activated," perhaps burning brighter than before—perhaps radiating a heat-like emission. The energy stream is followed, envisioning a continuous line from the center point of one *pentagram* to the start of the next as you move about the boundary of the ceremonial *nemeton* in a *deosil*—or "counter-clockwise" (banishing)—direction. At the end of the rite, the operator is surrounded by a band of four blazing interlocked *pentagrams*.

---

### The Lesser Banishing Ritual of the Pentagram

• The LBRP begins in the eastern quarter where the operator performs the *Middle Pillar Rite* and *Kabbalistic Cross Rite*. Then, while still in the east, the Sorcerer should trace the banishing pentagram, point to the center and intone: YHVH—"*yod-heh-vahv-heh.*"

• Then, in the south, the banishing pentagram is traced, the center is pointed to and the invocation is: ADNI —"*ah-doh-nye.*"

• In the western quarter: EHIH—"*eh-heh-yeh.*"

• And in the north: AGLA—"*ah-glah.*"

• Carry the *ray of light* back to the east, connecting to the first *pentagram*, then stand with outstretched hands to speak:

> *Before me, Raphael. Behind me, Gabriel.*
> *At my right hand, Michael. At my left hand, Auriel.*
> *Before me flames the pentagram.*
> *Above and below me shines the six-rayed star.*

---

While it is difficult to trace definitive origins for this specific version of the rite, it was immediately clear to early "Mardukite Chamberlains" that the most antiquated 4,000-5,000 year old Mesopotamian inspiration could be nothing else than the "*Incantation of Eridu*"—also called the "*Incantation of Enki*" or "*Incantation of Marduk.*" A few of the lines:—

*I am the priest in ERIDU.*
*I am the magician of BABYLON.*
*My spell is the spell of ENKI.*
*My incantation is the incantation of MARDUK.*
*SHAMMASH (Samas) is before me.*
*NANNA (Sin) is behind me.*
*NERGAL is at my right hand.*
*NINURTA is at my left hand.*
*ANU, above me, the King of Heaven.*
*ENKI, below me, the King of the Deep. . .*[*]

The "Watchtowers" are a very ancient concept inseparable from modern practices of ceremonial magic—and even some other magical traditions, such as *Wicca*, which chose to incorporate its use from early GD grimoires. Semantics are derived from ancient Mesopotamian "divisions" of command, stewarding and guardianship of specific *zones* and *domains*, as alluded to throughout mystical cuneiform tablet records concerning the "*Anunnaki*." Even the descriptive title "Watchers" is handed down from the Mesopotamian "*Igigi*"—"*those who see*"—but as related to the physical world, Watchtowers exist at the "*four corners*" of this cosmic dimension, guarded by figures sealing "*in*" (or "*out*") appropriate degrees of energy specific to the lower material domain that the Human condition is wired to experience as "typical."

Watchtowers are popularized in ceremonial magic from another GD rite within the same cycle as the LBRP—and as much as the LBRP is considered a "minor" method of "casting a circle" for *high magic* purposes, this other "*Watchtower Ceremony*"—or "*Watchtower Formula*" as it is sometimes called—was employed for all the more "advanced" GD operations and experiments, such as *Enochian magic*. There are some underground "societies" that make use of the rite for "initiation" and "installation" ceremonies.

---

[*]  See also *"The Complete Book of Marduk by Nabu"* or *"Practical Babylonian Magic"* by Joshua Free.

The "*Watchtower Formula*" follows a cumulative succession of the "rites" formerly provided and building upon the same *kabbalistic* formula. Divine Names used for this version are derived from the elemental or *Watchtower Tablets* of the *Enochian* system—which are meant to be present for this rite in the GD version. The Elemental, Watchtower or cross-quarter Gate tablets appear frequently in such rites—the fact they *are* originally "tablets" lends us a possible hint to their ancient Mesopotamian inspiration. All verbiage recited during the rite are direct passages from a treatise known among *esoteric* and "*Hermetic*" circles as the *Chaldean Oracles of Zoroaster*.* The rite employs traditional "ceremonial magic" rules and access to the "Elemental Tools" of ritual magick.

## *The Watchtower Ceremony-Formula*

The temple is arranged with a double circle. *Enochian tablets*—or elemental "Watchtower tablets"—are placed between the two circles at their appropriate directions. A banner, flag or other representation can be made and used in place of "tablets" proper. If employed for *Enochian* magic, then the "*Tablet of Union*" and "*Sigillum de Aemeth*" should also be present on the "altar."

- Perform the "Middle Pillar Rite"
- Perform the "Kabbalistic Cross Rite"
- Perform the "LBRP"

• Go and stand in the south, raise your sword, saying:

*Behold, all the phantoms have vanished and I see before me that sacred and formless fire that flames and consumes the hidden depths of the Universe and I hear the voice of the fire.*

---

* See also '*Tablet-0*' from the '*Mardukite Core*'—found within "*The Complete Anunnaki Bible*" (&tc.) by Joshua Free.

• Feel and see the sword radiate with fire, and say:

> Oh-ee-peh Teh-ah-ah Peh-doh-key [OIP TEAA PDOKE].
> In the names and letters of the Great Southern Quad-
> rangle, I invoke thee spirits of the Watchtower of the
> South.

• Go to the west and take up the sacred chalice; sprinkle
some of the water, saying:

> Now therefore I, a priest of fire, summon the lustral
> waters of the sea and hear the wrath of the waves
> upon the shore, the voice of the water now and ever-
> more.

• Feel the water element rising up within you, then say:

> Em-pehheh Ar-ess-el Gah-ee-oh-leh [MPH ARSL
> GAIOL]. In the names and letters of the Great Western
> Quadrangle, I invoke thee spirits of the Watchtower of
> the West.

• Go to the east and raise your dagger (or wand); strike the
air three times saying:

> My mind extends through the realm of air. In the
> formless air comes the vision and the voice, flashing,
> bounding, revolving, it whirls forth crying aloud.

• Feel and see the winds of the air element, swirling about
you as you say:

> Oh-roh Ee-bah Ah-oh-zod-pee [ORO IBAH AOZPI]. In
> the names and letters of the Great Eastern Quad-
> rangle, I invoke thee spirits of the Watchtower of the
> East.

• Go to the north and take up the pentacle; shake it in the air three times and say:

> I stoop down into a world of darkness, wherein lies
> unknown depths and Hades shrouded in gloom, de-
> lighting in senseless images; a black ever-rolling
> abyss, a voice both mute and void.

• Feel Earth beneath your feet; become very aware of the ground as you intone:

> Moh-are Dee-ah-leh Heh-keh-teh-gah [MOR DIAL
> HCTGA]. In the names and letters of the Great Northern
> Quadrangle, I invoke thee spirits of the Watchtower of
> the North.

• Finally, go to the east and proclaim:

> Holy art thou, Lord of the Universe. Holy art thou,
> whom Nature has not formed. Holy art thou, the In-
> finite and Mighty One, Lord of Light and of Darkness.

• When work is complete, the rite is ended with the LBRP.

# ENOCHIAN MAGICK OF JOHN DEE

Fascinated with astrology, *Dr. John Dee* (1527–1608) publicly predicted when *Queen Mary* would die and when it happened, he was imprisoned for using black magic to kill her. As her sister, *Queen Elizabeth I* ascended the throne, she released *Dee* making him her royal court astrologer. But, financial stress forced *Dee* to continue his earlier alchemical pursuits for the philosopher's stone—an interest that led him to the company of a young rogue-seer named *Edward Kelley*. As little as we truly know of *Dee*'s life, we know even less about his partner *Kelley*, except that they spent many years together allegedly conversing with angelic spirits, which led to the birth of the "*Enochian System of Magic*." *John Dee* excelled at "ceremonial magic," performed the rites as a practicing magician—while *Kelley* skryed into a crystal ball to decipher messages and letters of the *Enochian Alphabet*. A very complex ritual system was created—or channeled, depending on your opinion of its origins—including construction of the "*Sigillum Dei Aemeth*"—

The "*Enochian Tablet of Union*"—

The four "*Enochian Watchtower Tablets*"—

| r | Z | i | l | a | f | A | y | t | l | p | a |
|---|---|---|---|---|---|---|---|---|---|---|---|
| a | r | d | Z | a | i | d | p | a | l | a | m |
| c | z | o | n | s | a | r | o | Y | a | u | b |
| T | o | i | T | t | z | o | P | a | c | o | C |
| S | i | g | a | s | o | m | r | b | z | n | h |
| f | m | o | n | d | a | T | d | i | a | r | i |
| o | r | o | i | b | a | H | a | o | z | p | i |
| t | N | a | b | r | V | i | x | g | a | s | d |
| O | i | i | i | t | T | p | a | l | o | a | i |
| A | b | a | m | o | o | o | a | C | u | c | a |
| N | a | o | c | o | T | t | n | p | r | n | T |
| o | c | a | n | m | a | g | o | t | r | o | i |
| S | h | i | a | l | r | a | p | m | Z | o | x |

*Enochian Air Tablet*

| T | a | O | A | d | u | p | t | D | n | i | m |
|---|---|---|---|---|---|---|---|---|---|---|---|
| a | a | b | c | o | o | r | o | m | e | b | b |
| T | O | g | C | o | n | x | m | a | l | G | m |
| n | h | o | d | D | i | a | l | e | a | o | c |
| p | a | t | A | x | i | o | V | s | P | s | N |
| S | a | a | i | x | a | a | r | V | r | o | i |
| m | p | h | a | r | s | l | g | a | i | o | l |
| M | a | m | g | l | o | i | n | L | i | r | x |
| o | l | a | a | D | n | g | a | T | a | p | a |
| p | a | L | c | o | i | d | x | P | a | c | n |
| n | d | a | z | N | z | i | V | a | s | s | a |
| i | i | d | P | o | n | s | d | A | s | p | i |
| x | r | i | n | h | t | a | r | n | d | i | L |

*Enochian Water Tablet*

| b | O | a | Z | a | R | o | p | h | A | R | a |
|---|---|---|---|---|---|---|---|---|---|---|---|
| u | N | n | a | x | o | P | S | o | m | d | n |
| a | i | g | r | a | n | o | o | m | a | g | g |
| o | r | p | m | n | i | n | g | b | e | a | i |
| r | s | O | n | i | z | i | r | l | e | m | u |
| i | z | i | n | r | C | z | i | a | M | h | l |
| M | o | r | d | i | a | l | h | c | t | G | a |
| O | c | a | n | c | h | i | a | o | m | t |   |
| A | r | b | i | z | m | i | l | l | p | i | z |
| O | p | a | n | a | L | a | m | a | m | a | p |
| d | O | l | o | p | i | n | i | a | n | b | a |
| r | x | p | a | o | c | s | i | z | i | x | p |
| a | x | t | i | r | V | a | s | t | r | i | m |

*Enochian Earth Tablet*

| d | o | n | p | a | T | d | a | n | V | a | a |
|---|---|---|---|---|---|---|---|---|---|---|---|
| o | l | o | a | G | e | o | o | b | a | u | a |
| O | P | a | m | n | o | V | G | m | a | n | m |
| a | p | l | s | T | e | d | e | c | a | o | p |
| s | c | m | i | o | o | n | A | m | l | o | x |
| V | a | r | S | G | d | l | b | r | i | a | p |
| o | i | P | t | e | a | a | p | D | O | c | e |
| p | s | u | a | c | n | r | Z | i | r | Z | a |
| S | i | o | d | a | o | i | n | R | z | I | m |
| d | a | l | t | T | d | n | a | d | i | r | e |
| d | i | x | o | m | o | n | s | i | o | s | p |
| O | o | D | p | z | i | A | p | a | n | l | i |
| r | g | o | a | n | n | P | A | c | r | a | r |

*Enochian Fire Tablet*

And the "*Enochian Language*" as a whole—

| | Ceremonial | Cursive | | | Ceremonial | Cursive |
|---|---|---|---|---|---|---|
| **B (pe)** | | | | **P (mals)** | | |
| **C,K (veh)** | | | | **Q (ger)** | | |
| **G (ged)** | | | | **N (drun)** | | |
| **D (gal)** | | | | **X (pal)** | | |
| **F (orth)** | | | | **O (med)** | | |
| **A (un)** | | | | **R (don)** | | |
| **E (graph)** | | | | **Z (ceph)** | | |
| **M (tal)** | | | | **W,U,V (Vau)** | | |
| **I,J,Y (gan)** | | | | **S (fam)** | | |
| **H (nahath)** | | | | **T (gisa)** | | |
| **L (ur)** | | | | | | |

*The Enochian Alphabet*

...all of which are used to summon power of angelic spirits, communicate inter-dimensionally with these intelligences, or else conjure them to physical appearance. We may also see traces of *Gnostic* beliefs in the system, rites heavy with *kabbalistic* influences and other *Divine Names.*

The relationship between *Dee* and *Kelley* took a turn when *Kelley* informed him that a spirit named *Madimi* instructed them to share their wives. While it is said that *Dee* eventually gave into *Kelley*, no one knows what really transpired except that the unique magickal partnership ended abruptly. This background and *Kelley*'s wider reputation for mystical hoaxes has led many scholars to question the validity of the *Enochian System* In total. Any credibility of the system is probably derived more from *John Dee*'s contributions than *Kelley*'s.

> It is possible that over the centuries, much of the *Enochian System* has actually been "willed" into existence via the *thought-forms* representing powerful entities created by Sorcerers, practitioners and energetic relationships with later Magicians using the system.

As a derivative of *Kabbalistic* and other *Hermetic* systems, the *Enochian Tradition* represents a further evolution of post-Babylonian *Anunnaki* systems. In fact, in the past several decades, both the "*Enochian System*" and the "*Babili System*"* have been referred to by multiple authors as the "*Necronomicon*"—a semantic that even the modern *Mardukite* movement decided to carry for those who preferred it. What we do have in the *Enochian* methodology is not simply some arbitrary "Judeo-Christian" context for studying "angelic" phenomenon—it would seem to possess far greater *esoteric* or "Gnostic" applications—such as we might identify with those methods closely assimilating remnants of a post-Babylonian occult systemology, such as *Hermetics, Chaldean magic,* the *Persian magi, &tc.*

---

* See also *"Necronomicon: The Anunnaki Bible"* or *"The Complete Anunnaki Bible"* by Joshua Free.

As an effective "ceremonial" application, *Enochian Magic* requires a set of the aforementioned *Enochian Tablets*—the four *Watchtowers* and the *Tablet of Union*—a set of *magical weapons* or "elemental tools" previously "consecrated" to the high magical arts, and finally, the *Sigillum Dei Aemeth* appears, inscribed on a disc of wax or wood, which may replace the traditional ritual *pentacle* on the altar. The Sorcerer must also have a thorough understanding of the *Enochian Keys* (or *Calls*) used for invocations, in addition to memorizing hierarchical "roll calls" of angelic spirit names from within the system—*angels, astral kings* and other *guardians* evoked for these rites.

There are two forms of *Enochian Magic* studied and used in the contemporary systems and traditions of the "*New Age.*" The first is what we are already in the process of describing, which concerns evocation and spiritual interaction with *angelic* entities. A more advanced application of the system also exists, wholly dependent on an operator's ability to interact with the "*Astral Plane*" using "spirit vision." In the *Enochian* paradigm, semantics describing separations of dimensional veils are called *aethyrs*. Contrasting the *Babili* "Gate-system" and the "*sephiroth*" of the *Hebrew Kabbalah*, the *Enochian* system fragments the spiritual dimensions into thirty "aethyr zones." During ceremonial magic the operator calls for these *angelic spirits* from dimensions they presumably reside in.

"*Divine Names*"—or *words of power*—employed in the *Enochian System* are derived from "*Enochian Tablets*"—four *Watchtower* tablets and the *Tablet of Union*. Each "*Watchtower Tablet*" is appropriated to one of the cardinal directions or "quadrangles" (quarters) of the universe—but each of these tablets is also made up of four sections, divided by a "cross." A "cross-section" is also composed on each of the four smaller portions. In short, this means there are four watchtower tablets, each with a cross that separates four smaller sections—for a total of sixteen—that each contain a smaller cross. Philosophically, each of the four elemental tablets are subdivided into a microcosm of four elemental aspects.

The key to interpreting and correctly using the tablets requires understanding the quadrants. Whether used to consolidate a "Great Tablet" or differentiate the smaller sections of the "four" into "sixteen," the same formula key is used to divide sections into "elemental" quadrants:

---

AIR = upper left     WATER = upper right
EARTH = lower left     FIRE = lower right

---

Since each of the tablets are divided into "elemental quadrants," this provides for sixteen different elemental combinations—such as "earth of air" and so forth. The names of the "cross-angels"—as they are called in the *Enochian system*—are derived from the names distinguished by the smaller cross found within each quadrant. Names of the "senior-angels" are found in the larger cross that divides the four quadrants. Names and *sigils* of the "*aethyrs*" and their "governor" spirits are also taken from interpretations of the tablets—ritually tracing out "sigil-lines" that coincide with the pattern of letters as they appear on the tablets.

We have described energetic "tracing" of *signs* previously in the form of "pentagrams" for the *Lesser Banishing Ritual of the Pentagram,* but in the practice of *Enochian magic,* the "hexagram" is the preferred sign when related to "angelic spirits" and inter-dimensional communication. They are traced and envisioned in similar fashion as the magick circle is cast for rituals, pentagrams of the GD, or Signs of Portal in Druidism.

SATURN

Invoking Hexagram · Banishing Hexagram

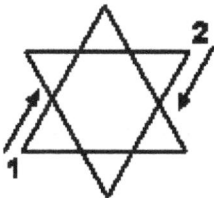

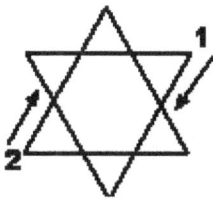

MOON

Invoking Hexagram · Banishing Hexagram

MERCURY

Invoking Hexagram · Banishing Hexagram

JUPITER

Invoking Hexagram · Banishing Hexagram

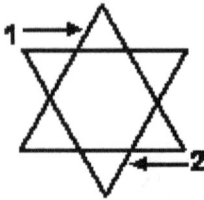

MARS

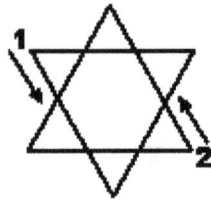

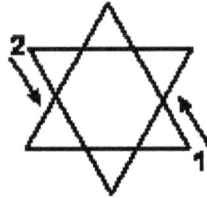

Invoking Hexagram   Banishing Hexagram

VENUS

Invoking Hexagram   Banishing Hexagram

The fundamental formula for *Enochian Magick* is as follows:—

Prerequisite Knowledge
 1. The name of the senior or angel to be evoked.
 2. The direction/Watchtower to face, using elemental
   correspondences.
 3. The Enochian Keys to be recited.
 4. The hierarchy or order of succession to be called. Use
   this order:
  a) Divine Name of the element,
  b) King,
  c) Seniors,
  d) Cross-Angel: six lettered,
  e) Cross-Angel: five lettered.
 5. The planetary-hexagram to be traced and the color to
   envision it (see *p. 31-32*).

Hints & Tips
 1. Except for Kings, the hierarchy needs only to be followed
until you reach the desired name.

2. A hexagram is traced only when you are evoking a Senior. (All six must be used to contact a King).

3. Use a pentagram if evoking Cross-Angels.

4. If evoking a Cross-Angel, you need only speak the names of the Seniors, though some Sorcerers prefer to trace all corresponding hexagrams.

5. Hexagrams are ruled by planetary forces, while the pentagrams are ruled by the elements.

<u>Order of Operations</u>

1. Enter the Body of Light and perform the Watchtower Ceremony.

2. Go to the appropriate direction/Watchtower and trace the hexagram(s) or pentagram envisioning it a color correspondent to the planet or element.

3. Intone the descending Enochian hierarchy from the designated element. When calling the Kings, you must intone each name of the Senior while synchronously tracing the appropriate hexagrams.

4. Repeat the name of the entity many times. Envision the name filling you and projecting from you. The spirit will appear in the traced star or some desired skrying speculum.

5. Perform the Lesser Banishing Ritual of the Pentagram (LBRP) when finishing the rite.

THE ENOCHIAN NAMES & WORDS OF POWER

<u>The Divine Names/Watchtowers</u>
  Air: Oro Ibah Aozpi (oh-roh ee-bah ah-oh-zod-pee)
  Water: Mph Arsl Gaiol (em-peh-heh ar-ess-el gah-ee-oh-leh)
  Earth: Mor Dial Hktga (moh-ar dee-al-el heh-keh-teh-gah)
  Fire: Oip Teaa Pdoke (oh-ee-peh teh-ah-ah peh-doh-key)

<u>Enochian/Elemental Kings</u>
  Air: Bataivah (bah-tah-ee-vah-heh)
  Water: Raagiosl (rah-ah-gee-ohs-el)
  Earth: Ikzhikal (ee-keh-zod-he-kah-el)
  Fire: Edlprnaa (ee-del-por-nah-ah)

<u>Enochian/Planetary Seniors</u>
[Order listed: Mars, Jupiter, Moon, Venus, Mercury and Sun.]
Air: Habioro, Aaozaif, Htmorda, Ahaozpi, Avtotar, Hipotga
Water: Srahpm, Saiinou, Laoaxrp, Slgaiol, Soniznt, Ligdisa
Earth: Laidrom, Akzinor, Lzinopo, Alhktga, Ahmllvk,
    Likiansa
Fire: Aaetpio, Adaeoet, Alnkdood, Aapdoke, Anadoin,
    Arinnap

<u>Enochian Keys/Calls for Kings and Seniors</u>
Air: 1, 2 and 3.
Water: 1, 2 and 4.
Earth: 1, 2 and 5.
Fire: 1, 2 and 6.

<u>Enochian Keys/Calls for Subordinate and Cross-Angels</u>
[Listed below are two names with the corresponding *Enochian Keys* to be used (in parenthesis). These entities represent qualities reminiscent to the alchemical breakdown of each of the elements into sixteen combinations.]

Air of Air: Idoigo, Aroza (3)
Water of Air: Lkalza, Palam (3 & 7)
Earth of Air: Aaioao, Oiiit (3 & 8)
Fire of Air: Aovrrs, Aloai (3 & 9)
Air of Water: Obgota, Abako (4 & 10)
Water of Water: Nelapr, Omebb (4)
Earth of Water: Maladi, Olaad (4 & 11)
Fire of Water: Iaaasd, Atapi (4 & 12)
Air of Earth: Angpol, Vnnax (5 & 13)
Water of Earth: Anaeem, Sonda (5 & 14)
Earth of Earth: Abalpt, Arbiz (5)
Fire of Earth: Ompnir, Ilpiz (5 & 15)
Air of Fire: Noalmr, Oloag (6 & 16)
Water of Fire: Vadali, Obava (6 & 17)
Earth of Fire: Volxdo, Sioda (6 & 18)
Fire of Fire: Rzionr, Nrzfn (6)

# THE ENOCHIAN KEYS & ANGELIC CALLS

Enochian Keys or Calls are used as incantation-prayers or invocations to the hierarchies of angels [Igigi] and the archangels [Anunnaki] in ceremonial applications of Enochian magic. They were divined by John Dee and Edward Kelley during the inception of the system from an 'angel' calling itself: Ave.

As with lore connected to other similar applications of what some might call the "Necronomicon," many esoteric students believe that Enochian Keys possess potential to unleash forces that are otherwise sealed from the time-space of human existence—the most condensed physical perception of reality. That being the case, the Enochian System seems like a prime candidate of the available "New Age" applications of Kabbalah for doing just that: inviting or summoning "alien" forces into our world! But, this is not something likely to happen by "accident," since any success with this system is dependent on the Sorcerer's "true" understanding and comprehension of related mysteries in Self-Honesty. In such a case, the Sorcerer is not simply inciting some "phenomenon," but as with the Babili system, is interested in developing a "true and faithful" relationship with inter-dimensional or "spiritual forces" that we encounter and communicate with in "magickal" work.

There is no reason to believe that the Enochian System is any closer, purer or better than the original Anunnaki Babili system—but Enochian secured high notoriety during the 20th century magical revival—accessible from the Golden Dawn and Aurum Solis literature. What follows are the translated English language "Enochian Keys" used for these methods.

### "The First Enochian Key"

I reign over you says the God of Justice, in power exalted above the firmaments of Wrath. In whose hands the Sun is as a sword and the Moon as a through-thrusting fire: Who measures your garments in the midst of my ventures and trussed you together as the palms of my hands: Whose seats I garnished with the Fire of Gathering: Who beautified your garments with admiration: To whom I made a law to govern the Holy Ones: Who delivered you with a rod and with the Ark of Knowledge. Moreover you lifted up your voices and swore obedience and faith to Him that lives and triumphs: Whose beginning is not nor can ever be: Which shines as a flame in the midst of your palaces and reigns among you as a balance of righteousness and truth. Move, therefore and show yourselves: open the mysteries of your creation. Be friendly unto me. For I am the servant of the same, your God, the true worshiper of the Highest.

### "The Second Enochian Key"

Can the Wings of Wind understand your voices of wonder, O you the Second of the First, whom the burning flames have formed within the depths of my jaws: Whom I have prepared as cups for a wedding or the flowers in their beauty for the chamber of righteousness. Stronger are your feet than the barren stone and mightier are your voices than the manifold winds. For you are becoming a building that is not, except in the mind of the All-Powerful. Arise, says the First. Move, therefore unto thy servants. Show yourselves in power and make me a strong seer of things, for I am descended from Him that lives forever.

### "The Third Enochian Key"

Behold, says your God. I am a circle on whose hands stand Twelve Kingdoms. Six are the seats of the living breath, the rest are sharp sickles or the horns of death, wherein the creatures of Earth are and are not, except by my own hands that also sleep and shall rise. In the First, I made you stewards and placed you on Twelve Seats of Government, giving unto every one of you the power over Four, Five and Six, the true ages of time: to the intent that the highest vessels and the corners of your government you shall work my power: pouring down the Fires of Life and increase continually upon the Earth. Thus you have become the skirts of justice and truth. In the names of the same, your God, lift up, I say to you. Behold, his mercies flourish and his name becomes mighty against us, as unto the initiates of the Secret Wisdom of your creation.

### *"The Fourth Enochian Key"*

I have set my feet in the South and have looked about me saying: Are not the thunders of increase numbered 33, which reign in the Second Angle? Under whom I have placed 9.639 whom none have numbered but One: In whom the Second beginning of things are and wax strong, which successively are the numbers of Time, and their powers are the First. Arise you Sons of Pleasure and visit the Earth: For I am the Lord your God which is and lives forever. In the name of the Creator, move and show yourselves as pleasant deliverers so that you may praise Him among the Sons of Men.

### *"The Fifth Enochian Key"*

The mighty sounds have entered the Third Angle and become as olives on the olive mount, looking with gladness upon the Earth and dwelling in the brightness of the heaves as continual comforters. Unto whom I have fastened 19 pillars of gladness and gave them vessels to water the Earth with all of her creatures: And they are the brothers of the First and Second, and the beginning of the own seats which are garnished with 69,636 continually burning lamps, whose numbers are as the First, the End, and the midway content of time. Therefore come and obey your creation. Visit us in peace and comfort. Include us the receivers of your mysteries. For why? Our Lord and Master is of the All-One.

### *"The Sixth Enochian Key"*

The spirits of the Fourth Angle are nine, mighty in the firmaments of water: the First has planted a torment to the wicked and a garland to the righteous: Giving unto them fiery darts to wash the Earth, and 7,699 continual workmen whose courses visit with comfort to the Earth, and are in government and continuance as the Second and the Third. Wherefore, come and follow my voice. I have talked of you and I move you in power and presence: Whose works shall be a song of honor and the praise of your *God* in your creation.

### "*The Seventh Enochian Key*"

The East is a house of virgins singing praises among the flames of the First glory, wherein the Lord has opened his mouth and they become 28 living dwellings in whom the strength of man rejoices and are appareled with ornaments of brightness, such a work that fascinates all creatures: Whose kingdoms and continuance are as the Third and Fourth, strong towers and places of comfort, the seat of mercy and continuance. O you servants of mercy, move, appear, and sing praises unto the Creator of All. And be might among us. For to this covenant is given power and our strength waxes strong in our comforter.

### "*The Eighth Enochian Key*"

The midday, the First, is as the Third Heaven made of 26 crystalline pillars, in whom the elders are becoming strong, which I have prepared for my own righteousness, says the Lord: Whose long continuance shall be as buckles to the Stooping Dragon and like unto the harvest of a widow. How many are there which remain in the glory of the Earth, which are, and shall not see death until this house falls and the Dragon sinks? Come away for the thousands have spoken! Come away for the Crown of the Temple and the robe of Him that is, was and shall be crowned King and divided. Come! Appear unto the terror of the Earth and unto our comfort and to those who are prepared.

### "*The Ninth Enochian Key*"

A mighty guard of Fire with two-edged swords flaming, which

have eight Vials of Wrath for Two times and a half, whose wings are wormwood and of the marrow of salt, have settled their feet in the West and are measured by their 9,996 ministers. These gather up the moss of the Earth as the rich man does guard his treasure. Cursed are they whose iniquities they are. In their eyes are millstones greater than the Earth and from their mouth runs seas of blood. Their heads are covered with diamonds and upon their hands are marble sleeves. Happy is he on whom they frown not. For why? The God of Righteousness rejoices in them. Come away and not your Vials, for the time is such that requires comfort.

### "The Tenth Enochian Key"

The thunders of judgment and wrath are numbered and are harbored in the North in the likeness of an Oak whose branches are 22 nests of lamentation and weeping laid up for the Earth, which burns night and day: And vomit out the heads of scorpions and active sulfur mingled with poison. These are the thunders that 5678 times (in the 24th part of your moment) roar with a hundred might earthquakes and a thousand times as many surges, which rest not, neither know any echoing time herein. One rock brings forth a thousand, as occurs in the hearts of men with their thoughts. Woe! Woe! Woe! Woe! Woe! Woe! Woe! Woe! Woe! Hear, I say, Woe! Be merciful to the Earth for her iniquity is, was and shall be great. Come away! But not your mighty sounds.

### "The Eleventh Enochian Key"

The mighty seat groaned aloud and there were five thunders, which flew into the East and the Eagle spoke and cried in a loud voice: Come away! And they gathered themselves together and became the House of Death, of whom it is measured, and it is 31. Come away! For I have prepared for you a place. Move therefore and show yourselves. Open the mysteries of your creation. Be friendly unto me, for I am a servant of the same, your God, who is the true worshiper of the Highest.

### "The Thirteenth Enochian Key"

O you swords of the South, which have 42 eyes to stir up the wrath of Sin: making men drunken and empty. Behold, the promise of God and His power, which is called amongst you a bitter string. Move and show yourselves. Open the mysteries of your creation. Be friendly unto me, for I am a servant of the same, your God, who is the true worshiper of the Highest.

### "The Fourteenth Enochian Key"

O you Sons of Fury, the legal heirs of the just, which sits upon 24 seats, vexing all creatures of the Earth with age, which have under them 1,636. Behold the Voice of God, the promise of Him, which is called amongst you Fury or extreme justice. Move, therefore and show yourselves. Open the mysteries of your creation. Be friendly unto me, for I am a servant of the same, your God, who is the true worshiper of the Highest.

### "The Fifteenth Enochian Key"

O thou, the Governor of the First Flame under whose wings are 6,739, which weave the Earth with dryness: Which knows the secret of the Great Name: righteousness, and the Seal of Honor. Move, therefore and show yourselves. Open the mysteries of your creation. Be friendly unto me, for I am a servant of the same, your God, who is the true worshiper of the Highest.

### "The Sixteenth Enochian Key"

O thou, Governor of the Second Flame, the House of Justice, who has your beginning in glory and shall comfort the just, who walks the Earth with 8,763 feet, which understands and separates the creatures. Great you are to the God of Conquest. Move, therefore and show yourselves. Open the mysteries of your creation. Be friendly unto me, for I am a servant of the same, your God, who is the true worshiper of the Highest.

### "The Seventeenth Enochian Key"

O thou, Governor of the Third Flame who wings are the thorns to stir up vexation. And who has 7,336 living lamps go ing before thee: Whose God is wrath in anger, bind up thy loins and take notice! Move, therefore and show yourselves. Open the mysteries of your creation. Be friendly unto me, for I am a servant of the same, your God, who is the true worshiper of the Highest.

*"The Eighteenth Enochian Key"*

O thou, the might light and burning flame of comfort, which opens the Glory of God unto the center of the Earth. I whom the 6,332 secrets of Truth have their abiding, which is called in your kingdom of Joy and not to be measured. Be thou a window of comfort unto me. Move, therefore and show yourselves. Open the mysteries of your creation. Be friendly unto me, for I am a servant of the same, your God, who is the true worshiper of the Highest.

# ADVANCED ENOCHIAN MAGICK & AETHYRS

In the Enochian Tradition, "*Aethyrs*" are the fragmented spiritual dimensions from which angelic spirits of the *Enochian System* are called. This lore is at the heart of one of the most advanced operations of *high magick* in the New Age, "*Rising on the Planes*," as executed in its entirety from a "Body of Light" using ceremonial magick. Accessing the *aethyrs* successfully relies on abilities to achieve "spirit vision" (or astral vision).

"Rising on the Planes" also requires astral passage through—or the attainment of—the first eighteen *Enochian Keys* before ceremonially executing the first of thirty cycles of *Call to the Aethyrs*. This "call" is the same for all *aethyrs* except that the title of each plane is replaced. Appropriate *sigils* of "angelic guardians/governors" of each *aethyr* may be carried as seals and "traced" while calling appropriate "Divine Names." The *Aethyrs* are aligned to fundamental elements, which determines the ritual direction to face and the "elemental/magickal weapon" used to trace the *sigils*.

Each *aethyr* must be accessed consecutively, though confusion occurs here since half of the traditions work from the thirtieth to the first and the other half follow opposite regimens. According to modern magical lore, once relationships are established between the practitioner and the "guardian spirits" of the first eighteen *Enochian Keys*, then operation of the *Call to the Aethyrs* will be sufficient to directly access these planes via astral "spirit vision." Names and *sigils* of aethyrs—that follow here—are derived directly from the *Enochian Tablets*.

| | | a) | b) | c) |
|---|---|---|---|---|
| 1 | LIL | | | |
| 2 | ARN | | | |
| 3 | ZOM | | | |
| 4 | PAZ | | | |
| 5 | LIT | | | |
| 6 | MAZ | | | |
| 7 | DEO | | | |
| 8 | ZID | | | |
| 9 | ZIP | | | |
| 10 | ZAX | | | |
| 11 | IKH | | | |
| 12 | LOE | | | |
| 13 | ZIM | | | |
| 14 | VTA | | | |
| 15 | OXO | | | |

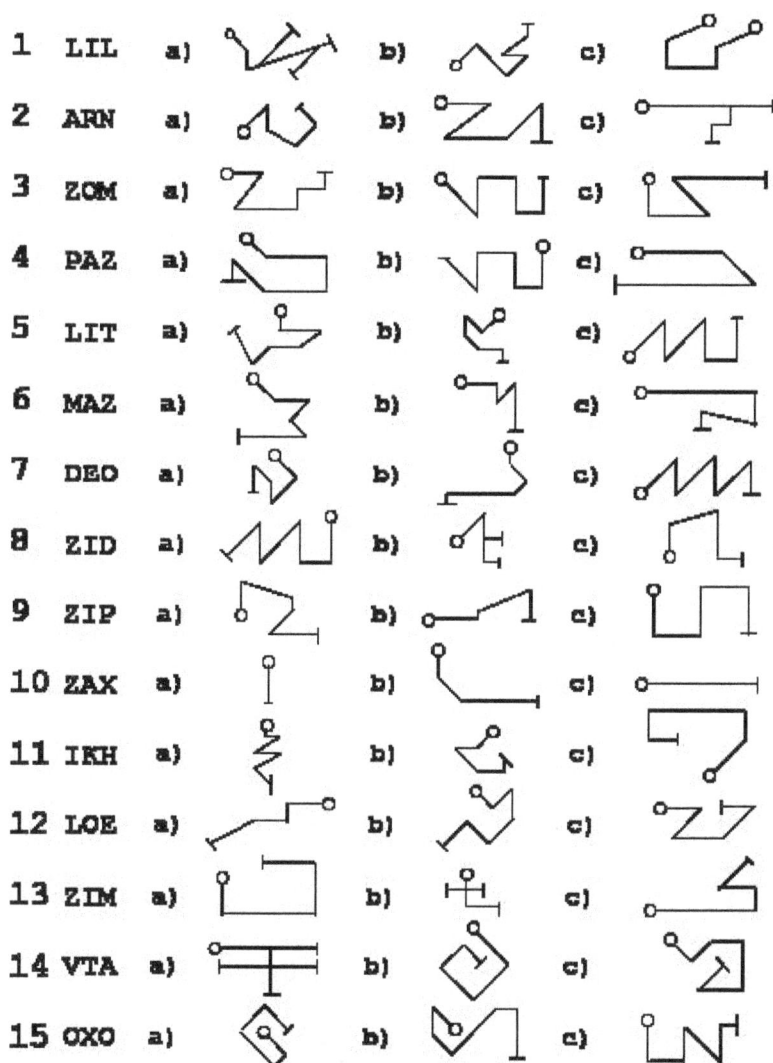

1. LIL (lee-lah) [water] Occodon, Pascomb, Valgars
2. ARN (ah-rah-noo) [water] Doagnis, Pacasna, Dialiva
3. ZOM (zoad-oh-me) [water] Samapha, Virooli, Andispi
4. PAZ (pah-zoad) [water] Thotanf, Axziarg, Pothnir
5. LIT (lee-tay) [water] Lazdixi, Nocamal, Tiarpax
6. MAZ (mah-zoad) [fire] Saxtomp, Vavaamp, Zirzird
7. DEO (day-oh) [fire] Obmacas, Genadol, Aspiaon

| | | | | | | | |
|---|---|---|---|---|---|---|---|
| 16 LEA | a) | | b) | | c) | | |
| 17 TAN | a) | | b) | | c) | | |
| 18 ZEN | a) | | b) | | c) | | |
| 19 POP | a) | | b) | | c) | | |
| 20 KHR | a) | | b) | | c) | | |
| 21 ASP | a) | | b) | | c) | | |
| 22 LIN | a) | | b) | | c) | | |
| 23 TOR | a) | | b) | | c) | | |
| 24 NIA | a) | | b) | | c) | | |
| 25 VTI | a) | | b) | | c) | | |
| 26 DES | a) | | b) | | c) | | |
| 27 ZAA | a) | | b) | | c) | | |
| 28 BAG | a) | | b) | | c) | | |
| 29 RII | a) | | b) | | c) | | |
| 30 TEX | a) | | b) | | c) | | d) |

8. ZID (zoad-ee-dah) [fire] Zamfres, Todnaon, Pristac
9. ZIP (zoad-ee-pay) [fire] Oddiorg, Cralpir, Doanzin
10. ZAX (zoad-ahtz) [union] Lexarph, Comanan, Tabitom
11. ICH (ee-kah-hey) [water] Molpand, Vanarda, Ponodol
12. LOE (loh-aye) [fire] Tapamal, Gedoons, Ambrial
13. ZIM (zoad-ee-me) [fire] Gecaond, Laparin, Docepax
14. VTA (vah-tah) [air] Tedoond, Vivipos, Ooanamb

15. OXO (ohx-oh) [air] Tehando, Nociabi, Tastoxo
16. LEA (lah-ay-ah) [air] Cocarpt, Lanaconi, Sochial
17. TAN (tah-noo) [air] Sigmorf, Aydropt, Tocarzi
18. ZEN (zoad-en) [air] Nabaomi, Zafasai, Yalpamb
19. POP (poh-pay) [air] Torzoxi, Abaiond, Omagrap
20. KHR (kay-hay-ray) [air] Zildron, Parziba, Totocan
21. ASP (ah-ess-pay) [air] Chirspa, Toantom, Vixpalg
22. LIN (lee-noo) [air] Oxidaia, Paraoan, Calzirg
23. TOR (toh-ray) [earth] Ronoamb, Onizimp, Zaxanin
24. NIA (nee-ah) [earth] Orcamir, Chialps, Soageel
25. VTI (vah-tee) [earth] Mirzind, Obvaors, Ranglam
26. DES (day-ess) [earth] Pophand, Nigrana, Bazchim
27. ZAA (zoad-ah-ah) [earth] Saziama, Mathula, Korpamb
28. BAG (bah-gee) [earth] Labnixp, Focisni, Oxlopar
29. RII (ree-ee) [earth] Vastrim, Odraxti, Gomziam
30. TEX (tehtz) [water] Taoagla, Gemnimb, Advorpt, Dozinal

---

### *Rising of the Planes (Enochian Aethyr Rite)*

1. Perform the "Watchtower Ceremony."
2. Face the appropriate direction based elemental correspondence of the aethyr.
3. Enter the Body of Light.
4. Recite the *"Key-Call of the Aethyr"* inserting the appropriate name of the aethyr.
5. Evoke the Angelic Guardians (governors) of the aethyr while tracing their sigils in the air visualizing them in an appropriate color (element based).
6. Leave the body using skrying or astral projection, allowing the astral body (or mental projection) to rise freely on that plane/aethyr.
7. Retrace the sigils in reverse to dismiss the spirits and perform the LBRP to complete the rite, negating any residual energies of the nemeton.

The "*Enochian Key to the Aethyrs*" is given here in two forms—in both *English* and *Enochian* languages. The English version provided is recommended for beginners—especially to this form of "magick." Practitioners should never intone incomprehensible words or formulas. All effective ritual and ceremonial symbolism must be determined and understood. The same applies to "*Divine Names.*" After the Sorcerer is more proficient with the *Enochian System* (and language),they may choose to use the Enochian version. The "*Call of the Aethyrs*" is referred to as the 19th-through-48th *Enochian Keys*, depending on the name of the *aethyr* inserted.

"*Enochian Key of the Aethyrs*"—(*English Version*)

The heavens that dwell in the (N. aethyr) are mighty in the parts of the Earth and execute the judgment of the Highest. Unto you it is said: Behold the face of your God, the beginning of comfort, whose eyes are the brightest in the heavens, which provided you for the government of Earth and her unspeakable variety, furnishing you with a powerful understanding to dispose all things according to the providence of him that sits at the Holy Throne and rose up in the beginning saying: The Earth, let her be governed by her parts and let there be division in her that the glory of her may be always drunken and vexed in itself. Her course, let it circulate with the heavens and as a handmaiden let her serve them. One season, let it confound another, and let there be no creature upon or with her one and the same. All her members let them differ in their qualities and let there be no one creature equal to another. The reasonable creature of Earth, and men, let them vex and weed out one another and their dwelling places. Let them forget their names. The work of man and his pompousness; let them be defaced. His buildings; let them become caves for the beasts of the field. Confound her under-standing with darkness. For why? I repent that I have made man. One moment, let her be known, in another moment, a stranger. Because she is the bed of a harlot and the dwelling place of him that is Fallen. O ye heavens arise! The lower heavens beneath you; let them serve you! Govern those that govern. Cast down such as fall. Bring forth those who increase and destroy the rotten. Let no place remain in one number. Add and diminish until the stars are numbered. Arise! Move! And appear before the covenant of his mouth, which he has sworn to us in his justice. Open the mysteries of your creation and make us partakers of the undefiled knowledge.

*"Enochian Key of the Aethyrs"*—(*Enochian version*)
Madriaax d s praf (N. aethyr) chis micaolz saanir od fisis bal zizras Iaida. Nonca gohulim: micma adoian mad, Iaod bliorb, soba ooaona chis Lucifitias Piripsol, ds abraassa nonif net aaib caosgi od tilb adphant damploz, tooatnoncfg Miadz Oma Irasd tol glo marb Yarry Id oigo od torxup Iaodaf gohol: Ca osga tabaord saanir od Christeos yrpoil tiobl busdir tilb noaln paid orsba od dodrmni zylna. Elzap tilb parm gi piripsax, od ta qurist booapis L hibm ovcho symp od Christeos ag toltorn mirc q tiobl L el. Tol paomd dilzmo as pian od Christeos ag L toltorn parach asymp. Cordziz, dodpal od didalz L smnad: of fargt bams omaoas. Conishra od avavox, tonug Orsca tbl noasmi tabges levithmong. Un chi omp tibl ors. Bagle? Modoah ol cordziz. L capimao izomaxip, od cacocasb gosaa. Baglem pi tianta a babalond, od foorgt teloc vovim. Madriax torzu! Oadviax orocho aboapri! Tabaori priaz artabas. Adrpan cors ta dobix. Lolcam priazi ar coazior, of Quasb Qting. Ripir paoxt sala cor. Vml od prdzar carcg aoiveae cormpt. Torzu. Zacar. Od zamran aspt sibsi butmona, ds surza ti-aballa Odo cicle qaa, od ozozma plapli Iadnamad.

# NECROMANTIC MAGICK & CONJURATIONS

The magickal ability to "conjure" or "evoke" spiritual entities to physical appearance is perhaps one of the most advanced long-sought uses of ceremonial magick conducted by Adept Magicians. Fortunately, Sorcerers may call on the powers extended by entities without waiting for conducive conditions for spirits to expend unnecessary energy on a physical apparition. Many occult masters consider the forcing of a spiritual manifestation of this sort as especially unwise. It is better to use a black mirror or other "*skrying*" medium and meet the spirit on the Astral Plane using "spirit vision." This helps to ensure the Sorcerer's safety and conserve energy used to accomplish a task—which is not the "summoning" of the spirit itself, but rather their metaphysical signature abilities. It is therefore not advised to focus energy on physical manifestations of a spirit—but instead concentrate on connecting with the actual raw energy current/ray requested from the entity.

Historically, the relationship between Sorcerers or Magicians and the hierarchies of spirits and angels they "command" is a stressed one. Any simple analysis of the classical "grimoires" from the Medieval and Renaissance periods will reveal this— where Magicians frequently make harsh demands of spirits, sometimes threatening them, and even cursing them by the Divine Names if they do not readily appear. These same Sorcerers would spend an unending amount of energy trying to protect themselves from the same energies they were calling by coercion. A rational and ethical wizard will find such a relationship absurd and counterproductive to the *Great Work* or journey of true magic—the Path to Ascension.

Assuming the primary goal is a "physical apparition"—if after three request and thirty minutes have passed without results, do not despair, *but* end the rite immediately. Close with the LBRP and dismiss the spirit as though it did arrive but not appear—and make notes of the conditions and your experience. You may or may not decide to try the same rite again under different conditions—weather, lunar phases, seasons, &tc.

True Magicians and Mystics are aware of the universal oneness (or wholeness) present within and as all seen and unseen existence. Those Wizards on the Self-Honest path understand the Cosmos and "spirit world" differently than what is generally represented in traditional "grimoires" or other occult instruction. When accessed via "astral vision" or the "aether" in ceremonial magick, spirits so commanded are an integral part of ourselves—and it is the fragmentation or individualization of our existence from Source that allows us to perceive these other beings as separate. These states of separation and union are bridged—as with all energetic interaction—by the path of "communication," and this bridge is usually represented in rituals as some type of catalyst—whether it is a pool of natural water or the construction of some type of blackened mirror surface (which is easily accomplished by painting the under side of glass with black paint). The "Key of Solomon" *grimoire* recommends the construction of the "Triangle of Solomon"—a triangular plate of cedar wood with a circular blackened mirror in the center, surrounded by the name "MI-CHA-EL" (in three portions) and on each of three sides of the triangle, a word: TETRAGRAMMATON, ANAPHAXETON, and PRIMUMATON

When the "Hermetic Order of the Golden Dawn" (GD) performed evocations, they did so in the most elaborately cast circles. Enochian and Elemental Tablets are used, along with the Tablet of Union. The LBRP, Watchtower Ceremony, &tc. are used in succession as opening rites. The pentagrams and hexagrams are traced in appropriate quarters—depending on the nature of the spirit being evoked, while simultaneously calling out for them. Some grimoires and Enochian methods suggest working through a certain spiritual "pantheon" or hierarchy of spirits, to summon the powers of a specific one.

Holy Names are usually called in out as a series of syllables, based on the phonetics of their native language. The act of writing phonetically extends back to ancient Mesopotamian languages and the original systematized writing scripts represented by *cuneiform* signs. When intoning "Divine Names" or other "spirit names" for evocation, the Sorcerer clears their mind and focuses on each toned utterance (syllable) and its significance as it is spoken, summoning generated energy with inhalations, and exhaling a "*Ray*" or specific vibration. Some have suggested that the characters (letters) of names themselves should be visualized in their respective alphabets as they are intoned, which is usually Enochian or Hebrew in these types of magick—though the premise could just as easily apply to other Celtic or Norse alphabets, and in the case of Mesopotamian Neopaganism, even cuneiform signs.

In the *Key of Solomon*, the Sorcerer follows a basic formula of praying to the Source of All—invoking the Tetragrammaton and the (Gnostic-Hermetic) Divine Names, then, from a Body of Light speaking a conjuration specifically at the entity. Hundreds of prayers and conjurations may be accumulated from the various grimoires. However, Abraham the Jew—the scion of the *Sacred Book of Magic of Abramelin the Mage*—recommends that wizards write their own prayers. In many instances, the conjurations found in classical grimoires can be in excess of a dozen paragraphs long. The *kabbalistic* conjuration included here is derived from the *Key of Solomon*.

### The Great Conjuration of Solomon-the-King

I conjure ye spirit *N.* by the power, virtue and wisdom of the spirit and the Name of God, by the undefiled knowledge, by the mercy, strength, greatness and unification of God; and by the Divine Name EHEIEH, in which all other Holy Names derive their existence. I conjure ye spirit N. by YOD, the name representing the simplicity and Divine Unification of God and all Creation. I conjure ye spirit N. by the Tetragrammaton: YOD-HEH-VAHV-HEH ELOHIM, which expresses the might and majesty of God and all of creation. I conjure ye spirit N. by the strength and mercy of EL. I conjure ye spirit N. by the omnipotent name ELOHIM GIBOR. I conjure ye spirit N. by the Divine Name, ELOAH VA-DAATH, the God of Israel. I conjure ye spirit N. by ELOHIM TZA-BAOTH, the God revealed in undefiled knowledge. I conjure ye spirit N. by the name EL ADONAI TZABAOTH, the God of armies. I conjure ye spirit N. by SHADDAI EL CHYE, the Divine Name of the Living God. Finally I conjure ye spirit N. by ADONAI MELEKH, the name invoked by Joshua. Yes, spirit N. I conjure you here by all of the Holy Names of God. Move now from your darkness and show yourself by the power of the Source of All Being and Creation.

## DEATH, ENERGY & MAGICK

Modern society primarily perceives death from a religious perspective—thus our attitudes toward it are reflected from what a person is socially conditioned to believe. This usually is reduced to two flavors: firstly, that one might fear death because it is the end of all things to them and an invitation into non-existence; or, one might view death as a means to a further end and an invitation into some "heavenly" abode. No one is indifferent about death, except lower-evolved Humans, and no one wants to believe that they are wrong on the subject. Most true esoteric occult doctrines express continuity of life in perpetuity, generally following a unfoldment of spiritual evolution. As the wise have once said: "What is there to *fear* in death?—when was I ever *less* by dying?"

While the concept of "death" is easily glorified negatively or conjured into gruesome imagery for popular (or unpopular) media, a clear understanding and familiarity is critical before a Sorcerer can expect to have practical applications of "death energy" in magickal practices.

"Death," is not an absolute negation of spiritual entities. It is a "state" or "condition" best described as a "threshold" or "in between" twilight of one aspect of existence. It should not be taken lightly, nor should it be feared, however it is respect of *Life* conditions that progresses us on the path. As any other "transition" or "transformation," physical death is a bridge from one vehicle/state to another. This process should not be hastened along in any way—for it is the condition of Life that we are here to experience and nurture appropriately. But as a widely observed phenomenon of transformation for all life and existence, the iconic archetype of "death" is inseparable from themes and practices of certain esoteric occult facets. It would seem even our mystical traditions are derived from a respect for ancestors we might honor at *Samhain*, or even those "intelligences" contacted through spiritual evocation.

## HIGH NECROMANTIC MAGICK

The combined energies of light and death make life—and so those who have been drawn to, for example, the ways of the *Westgate Necromantic Tradition*, carry a kinship, magnetic resonance or affinity with the "death current"—or death energy. These practices *do not* condone necrophilia or desecration in any way. Working with death energy through "high necromantic magick" is also different from *necromancy* or spirit evocation—which is diving information from dead spirits or conjuring them in ceremonies, usually for the same purpose.

Some of the foremost underground leaders in these practices, including Leilah Wendell, who once maintained the Westgate Death Museum of New Orleans, suggest direct contact with death in order to align familiarity with it. Many people are looked at as simply "crazy" for possessing such a fixation on "death" icons and motifs—and often many bring this energy to a "dark" place because they "crave" left-handed darker energies in their life for the wrong reasons. Such individuals are likely to more visibly display and emphasize this type of subcultural theme and lifestyle, attracting a lot of attention and setting a precedent for many what many people regard as a stereotype of occult practitioners.

Past cultures maintained increased appreciation for death, ancestors, bloodlines and care-taking (for elders)—as well as extraordinary rites and incantations said over a person who is dying or recently has died, which is especially evident in various "*Books of the Dead.*" It is therefore not uncommon to find "death energy magicians" working in mortuary professions and/or spending time at cemeteries, &tc.* Self-initiation in the archaic *Westgate* tradition required a solitary evening alone for meditation within an inhabited crypt or mausoleum (called a "death watch"). Leilah Wendell has suggested the "amethyst" stone and "jasmine" essence/incense best resonate "death energy" for meditation and magick.

---

* See also *"The Vampyre's Handbook"* by Joshua Free.

# THE NECRONOMICON
# & MESOPOTAMIA

At some place, some time, you first heard the word:

**NECRONOMICON**

More than simply a book imagined by a fantasy horror writer, or the product of some intensive Mesopotamian investigations in the 1970's, the Necronomicon is a piece of human consciousness, a primordial archetype that has existed in the backwaters of the mind for thousands of years. "New Age" revivals of ancient paganism and earth oriented spirituality, Druidry and magick are a natural response: the state of the world is in demand for a complete shift in human awareness. And while H.P. Lovecraft may have been alluding to such a tradition nearly one hundred years ago (even if only subconsciously) and the 1960's witnessed a gigantic practical rebirth of such traditions, it was in the late 1970's that a separate but synchronous mainstream awakening occurred: renewed interest in antiquated Sumerian and Babylonian mysteries, specifically emphasizing the role of *Anunnaki*, "Great Gods" who once roamed the Earth and became figures of our ancient mythologies all around the globe.

Since the arrival of the *Necronomicon* by "Simon" and Zecharia Sitchin's *"Twelfth Planet"* in the late 1970's, the Mesopotamian mysteries have increasingly become a focus of underground occultism. They have, at least in part, helped to shine some light on the "true tradition" of the Ancient Mystery School that has otherwise eluded pop-culture mainstream New Age metaphysics. A high priest or Druidess might obtain some decent recognition with the publication of their coven's "Book of Shadows," or a television psychic goes on to make a career leading lonely housewives "into the light"—it is the "Simonian" *Necronomicon* that stands alone over the past decades as the leading occult bestseller, with more than a million copies in circulation... not including those which have been unofficially circulated.

There is no logical reason to give into this whole idea that the book itself will "cause" someone to go crazy or give in to criminal activities, as has been suggested in the past. We can appreciate the idea of "triggers on the psyche," but someone who already operating in a state of "clear mind" will not actively respond to passive stimulus—movies, pictures, books, &tc.—unless a predilection is already there.[*]

Simon's *Necronomicon* only alluded to a tradition, perhaps the most ancient tradition. The work was not "ahead of its time," but was instead "lagging behind its time," seeking to preserve, from the memory of an allegedly Arabic author, the lore and traditions of a dying Babylonian priesthood, but secondhand at best. The work is then transferred into the Greek format by which the "editors" of the Simonian edition are said to have used for their version. This would make some sense, since "sigil magick" paramount in that edition is "Hermetic"—not necessarily ancient Mesopotamian.

Figures appearing in our ancient mythologies as "Gods"—including divine encounters referred to in the Old Testament—were of a common origin, called *Anunnaki* by some, an important key to understanding the convoluted evolution of the original tradition that developed into the variegated systems now bursting from the New Age. For example, the ancient Mesopotamian tradition echoed across the Danube River of mainland Europe by a group called the "Tuatha d'Anu" or

---

[*] See also *"Necronomicon Revelations-or-Crossing to the Abyss"*—also available in the anthology, *"Gates of the Necronomicon: The Secret Anunnaki Tradition of Babylon"* edited by Joshua Free.

"Children of Anu" into what we know as "Druidism." And what's more, if all of these concepts do center around some type of alien inter-dimensional intelligences, then certainly the foundations of all modern religious, mystical and even anthropological lore are in serious need of reevaluation. Such efforts have been put forth in the past decade by the modern Mardukite "New Thought" movement that includes themes of Druidry and Mesopotamian Neopaganism, which shines a new light on these mysteries and in a time when they may be best received.*

## NECRONOMICON: THE ANUNNAKI BIBLE

"Necronomicon: The Anunnaki Bible" (by Joshua Free) was re-searched and developed to validate the reconstruction of a "Mardukite" movement—a basis for mystical priesthoods and and the Ancient Mystery School of Babylon and Egypt, illu-minating the distant source for a diverse array of modern practical systems. As such, Necronomicon: The Anunnaki Bible is presented to the public by the modern Mardukites as a pious volume of the oldest written records on the planet, providing a fresh boost of Self-Honesty to human consciousness concern-ing "The Book"—one that is not merely shroud in some gruesome sophomoric gothic fantasy horror.

The original Mardukite source book anthology—"Necronomi-con: The Anunnaki Bible"—is a masterpiece of Mesopotamian magic, spirituality and history, providing a grand symphony of correlated materials drawn from the most ancient Sumeri-an and Babylonian writings, detailing esoteric cosmology, the development of human history and descriptions of world or-der—all of which are used to maintain spiritual and physical control of humanity. These raw underground materials have shaped the existence of man's beliefs and traditions for thou-sands of years—right from the heart of the Ancient Near East.

---

* "Necronomicon: The Anunnaki Bible" or "The Complete Anunnaki Bible: A Source Book of Esoteric Archaeology" by Joshua Free.

## THE ESOTERIC BABYLONIAN MYTHOS

In a time before man, the first dragon—TIAMAT—emerged from the primordial sea to produce life.* *Tiamat* ruled the Ancient Ones—a reptilian race of beings representing origins of the "Dragonmind" in the human condition—the "craving to know" and unquenchable thirst for material power.

Eventually an opposition force emerges—the *Anunnaki* or Elder Gods—the systematizers of the cosmos. As described in the Babylonian "Epic of Creation"—called the *"Enuma Eliš"*—the Anunnaki god *Marduk* is raised to supremacy (empowered by the Anunnaki Wizard, *Enki)* among the Elder Gods. He defeats the "chaos dragon" *Tiamat*, and orders the Universe. Slaying the beast in two: he uses half of her body to form the Heavens, and the other half to form the Earth.

Empowered by the "Tablet of Destinies," *Marduk* fashions a "Gate" to lock out the Ancient Ones from this world—and it is sometimes called the "Gate to the Outside" in esoteric lore. It cannot be opened except by one of the "Sons of Man"—and the Seal of the Gate is known as the "Elder Sign." It is further written that *Marduk* and *Enki* upgraded a race of Humans to keep watch over the Gate, so that the Ancient Ones would never come to rule again this plane. They compiled magickal lore for the Watchers of the Gate—including protections and exorcisms if the Ancient Ones ever seeped out, or if their "worshipers" attempted to open the Gate. This magickal tradition came to be known by some as the *Necronomicon*.

In Simon's *"Necronomicon,"* the term *"zonei"* is applied to the planets of fixed orbits—a schema that is paramount for defining the Gate positions and domains of the Celestial hierarchy of the original Mesopotamian pantheon. Planets visible from Earth become the primary focus of spiritual tradition and religious astrology in Babylon, which is still observed today.

---

* See also *"Draconomicon: The Book of Ancient Dragon Magick"* by Joshua Free.

Mesopotamian tradition—and both *Simon's* and the Mardukite recensions of the *Necronomicon*—emphasize *Anunnaki* figures of the original Celestial pantheon, which were later adopted into all mythologies under their own specific cultural themes and languages. It is clear, as a pointed fact reflected throughout modern Mardukite literature, that ancient Mesopotamian records reveal a source or origin for lingering modern spiritual knowledge. The *Anunnaki*—"Anunaki" or "Annunaki"— have been interpreted several ways over the past centuries, including "judges decreeing the fate on earth" (academic); "from heaven to earth came" (Sitchin); "star-dragons" (de Vere); and the *Elohim* of Hebrew scripture. Furthermore, a subordinate race of "Watchers" or the *Igigi* ("those who see") are also found in related traditions—most typically equated to the "fallen angels" in contemporary paradigms. Esoteric Hebrew lore explains how Shamihaza, a leader of the Watchers, descends to earth with two-thirds of these angels—and concurrently in Mesopotamian lore, "Shamgaz" brings 200 of the 300 *Igigi* to Earth to take "Daughters of Men" as wives.

**FINAL THOUGHTS—AN INVITATION**

Prior to the modern Mardukite inception in 2008—when the *"Sorcerer's Handbook"* of "Merlyn Stone" was first developed— the primary benchmark for Mesopotamian Neopaganism was exclusively Simon's *"Necronomicon."* This has since changed, demonstrating progress of the 21st century New Age efforts as reflected in the "Mardukite Core" library of materials. For those interested in further pursuing the progressive "magickal path" presented in this book, the current editors strongly suggest the Mardukite anthologies by Joshua Free, currently available in 10th Anniversary Collector Edition hardcovers as *"Necronomicon: The Anunnaki Bible," "Gates of the Necronomicon: The Secret Anunnaki Tradition of Babylon"* and *"Necronomicon Anunnaki Grimoire: A Manual of Practical Babylonian Magick."*

# LOST BOOKS OF MERLYN STONE

# THE SORCERER'S NOTEBOOK*

### CRYSTAL POWER

The "Atlantean Power Rod" is constructed from a hollow copper tube of pipe—with a copper cap at one end. The quartz crystal (1 to 3 inches long) is placed at the uncapped end. The outer surface of the rod may be wrapped in leather. Combat rods are often wrapped in black; healing rods are traditionally blue, red and/or green. The crystal power rod is used to direct currents of energy through visualization. Healing rods may have crystals at both ends.

Atlantean Crystal Headbands help to amplify psychic/psionic (Mental) powers. Take a sheet of thin copper, cut and bend to form a band. A silver disc or coin about two inches in diameter is fastened to the front of the band—coinciding with the "Third Eye." A quartz with a flat end is then affixed to the disc. You may wish to punch holes at each end of the copper and attach leather cords so it may be tied around your head.

### INFLUENCING OTHERS

The magick used to manipulate others to see in your favor is a part of personal magnetism. There are innumerable ways to reinforce or strengthen personal magnetism in general. This rite is specifically designed to influence a specific person in

---

* Commissioned in 1998 by the "Outer Court" (or "Outer Circle") of the "*Elven Fellowship Circle of Magick*" (EFCOM) in Denver, which was integrated into their "Book of Shadows" officially in 1999.

the direction of agreement with you in a specific aspect. A greater energetic link (proximity, familiarity, involvement) promotes higher success—meaning, it is not advised to use this rite to attempt influence of an employer to give you a raise, when you don't even work for that person and they don't even know you exist. It is suggested to practice this rite at night, before sleeping—and when you believe the other person may be sleeping or dreaming.

---

### Influencing Others—Astral & Energy Work

• Lie comfortably on your back;
• Progressively relax the whole body;
• Enter the "Body of Light" and Astral;
• Use meditative breathing for three to five minutes;
• Intone the name "IAO" (*properly...*) three times;
• Visualize the person you wish to influence;
• Visualize your own Astral "Shell";
• Merge their Astral Form with your "Shell";
• Feel as if your Astral Form is occupying the other person's body;
• Hold this realization for three to five minutes;
• Think of the thoughts/images you want them to have to be in a state of agreements—using "I" statements repeatedly;
• Separate your "Shell" from their Astral Form;
• Abruptly dismiss the visualization and perform any personal grounding exercises.

---

## "RITE OF THE BLADE"

Before energies of the circle have been raised, each member undergoes a quick but meaningful initiation into the circle. The East member (or leader) stands at the eastern zone of the circle's boundaries and the members are lined up (elementally) clockwise, behind the South member.

The East member holds the black-handled dagger with their right hand to the left breast of the South member. His left hand is on the South member right shoulder.[*]

> East: *It would be better for you to rush upon this blade then to enter our circle with fear in your heart. How do you enter?*

> South: *With perfect love and perfect trust.*

> East: *I welcome you to the circle as a 'free person'* (handing off the dagger to the South member).

> South (to the West): *It would be better for you to rush upon this blade then to enter our circle with fear in your heart. How do you enter?*

> West: *With perfect love and perfect trust.*

> South: *I welcome you to the circle as a 'free person'* (handing off the dagger to the West member).

> West (to the North): *It would be better for you to rush upon this blade then to enter our circle with fear in your heart. How do you enter?*

> North: *With perfect love and perfect trust.*

> West: *I welcome you to the circle as a 'free person'* (handing off the dagger to the North member).

The North member hands the black-handled dagger to the leader—or continues initiating other members of the Circle. Once this is completed, the leader (or acting *Master*) may begin the formal "Casting of the Circle"—and the opening of the chapter (or lodge) to the proper Grade/Degree.

---

[*]   The ritual is performed similar to what is seen in the movie, *The Craft.*

## AN ELVEN-DRUID CURSE

To curse another; obtain an *oak leaf* and *four black candles*. The "oak leaf" will symbolize your enemy and the four candles are to surround it at each "direction." It is best if the leaf has their name written on it in charcoal.

> Then intone: *Behold, saith me—the mighty voices of my vengeance smash the stillness of the air and I am a master of annihilation. May the powers of the four fighters—Esras* (light the east candle), *Uscias* (light the south candle), *Semius* (light the west candle) *and Morfessa* (light the north candle)—*come and fix this curse upon thee, o' ___ who has caused me anguish.*

Light the leaf on fire and visualize your enemy burning.

## THE GREAT TREE RITE

> Leader: *We are here to give witness to the unity and strength of the magic circle, this mandala of love most holy. We, the Druids, the Children of Light, are at one with thee, O Sacred Tree. You, who stands as an eternal symbol of the Circle of Light and Life. You, who represent our eternal link with the ever-present Source. We honor and imitate you as the perfect living specimen of the Source of All Being and Creation. We watch you as you progress through the sacred Earth Year.*

> North: *The beginnings, middles, and ends of the sacred Earth Year.*

> East: *The balance and equinox forces of the sacred Earth Year.*

> South: *Tonight (today) we coven together, man and tree, acknowledging the Sacred Grove.*

> West: *We celebrate the strength, love, and unity of the*

*Sacred Grove, and in that celebration we honor the central icon of its existence: The Great Tree.*

<u>East</u>: *From the Eastern Winds we are granted a season of growth, as the sun emerges in the spring.*

<u>South</u>: *From the Southern Flame we are granted a season of fullness, as the sun warms the summer.*

<u>West</u>: *From the Western Waves we are granted a season of transformation with the shifting tides of autumn.*

<u>North</u>: *From the Firmness of Northern Ground we are granted a season of stability, self-reflection, and stillness, as the Earth hibernates and is renewed through winter.*

<u>Leader</u>: *The calendrical month ___, the Oghamic month of the ___ tree in the ancient Druid's calender.* [Traces the Oghamic rune in the air.] *May the blessing of ___, and the corresponding energies of ___ be projected forth into our auric light.*

---

### THE GREAT TREE RITE—OGHAM KEYS

January: Alder Tree, *Fearn*, protection and power.
February: Willow Tree, *Saille*, healing & enchantment.
March: Ash Tree, *Nuin*, protection and peace.
April: Hawthorn Tree, *Huatha*, love and purity.
May: Oak Tree, *Duir*, strength and leadership.
June: Holly, *Tinne*, purification and balance.
July: Hazel Tree, *Coll*, intuition and creativity.
August: Vine, *Muin*, meditation and prophecy.
September: Ivy, *Gort*, protection and growth.
October: Reed, *Ngetal*, intense energy and direct action.
13th:* Elder Tree, *Ruis*, completion and reflection.
November: Birth Tree, *Beith*, fertility and growth.
December: Rowan Tree, *Luis*, strength and insight.

---

\* *"13th Month"*—A *"Blue Moon"* or Samhain (*Oct.31-Nov.2*) or else some other *"New Years"* period to synchronize the luni-solar calendar.

<u>East</u>: *May the Sacred Grove and the Great Tree grant us the strength of the ancient Druids.*

<u>South</u>: *We hereby swear (reaffirm) our Guardianship of Gaea, the Sacred Grove, the Great Tree, and all life in Creation.*

<u>West</u>: *May the gentle rains bless all of Creation, nurturing and giving life, forever and always.*

<u>Leader</u>: *The entangled roots of the Great Tree shall live deep within our being, offering nourishment and stability to all of its faithful guardians.*

<u>North</u>: *And in between the roots and branches, we stand as the Guardians, the Keepers of the Earth, we who live in imitation of Oak Trees.*

<u>East</u>: *Our branches reach into the same sky proving that ascension is the purpose and goal of all life.*

<u>South</u>: *Great Universal Spirit, beings inhabiting this Sacred Tree, we stand here as your worthy guardians, and Keepers of the Earth and her mysteries.*

<u>West</u>: *May we grow to become our full potential from the seedlings we now are. May seeds plant in the world, bloom and flourish, spreading the true beauty and love of the Source of All, shared by all those receptive.*

<u>Leader</u>: [Traces Ogham sign on the tree; then knocks three times lightly on the trunk, intoning the name of the tree, perhaps in Celtic language, with each knock.] *O Great Tree, you are hereby awakened by the Druids of the ancient and ineffable knowledge.*

<u>North</u>: *May the ground that covers the roots, forever and always be blessed with all that is good and holy. May all of creation grow as the trees in the forest, each beautiful in their own uniqueness, yet*

*still sharing the same Earth in which too spread roots and call home.*

Leader: *We are united in our strengths, our faith, our love, and our trust. Ours in the bond that must endure all other bonds. The Truth Against the World.*

All: *The Truth Against The World.*

Leader: *Through True Knowledge, Power.*

All: *Through True Knowledge, Power.*

Leader: *So mote it be.*

## CRYSTAL CAPACITORS

In addition to "Astral Light" gear—and physical crystal power rods and headbands—crystal capacitors may be used to generate an "artificial" vortex of earth energy. Quartz crystals beneath the ground, either naturally or intentionally buried, adjust vibrations of the terrain. Portable crystal capacitors may be used above ground as needed to create a *psionic* force-field. In small quantities they should be set at each of the four cardinal (elemental) directions and a larger one in the center to focus surrounding energy. A basic crystal capacitor resembles part of a crystal headband—a single determination crystal with a flat base mounted on a silver disc to copper.

## THE ASTRAL TEMPLE WITHIN

This rite is to cleanse the *Inner Temple* (*Astral Temple*) and/or as preparation for other *energy work*.

1. Sit comfortably, hands and feet not crossing.
2. Visualize an atmosphere of white cleansing energy.

3. Begin inhaling it into your body.
4. Allow it to wash through you.
5. Now breathe in clear air.
6. As you breathe in clear air, see and feel it pushing out the impurities, the cleansing air is purified.
7. These impurities fall to your feet and are pushed into the ground.
8. Intone: *O Forces of White Light, Radiant Starfyre, cleanse my Inner Temple of impurity. Cleanse me now. Make me pure. So must it be.*
9. Visualize the white light energy returning around you.
10. Feel and see it perform a protective aura around your body, beginning with the head and moving down.

## BLUE CROWN—HEALING LIGHT

Concerning the Rays of *Starfyre*, the color blue is indicative of healing, meta-spiritual wholeness and vitality. For thousands of years, mystics have used this type of energy work towards healing and to promote an aura of tranquility and peace. A variation of this technique may be used to conjure the "Astral Armor of the Blue Flame."

1. Activate the *Inner Temple*.
2. Create an atmosphere of azure blue.
3. Inhale this energy ray and light.
4. Fill your being with it.
5. Intone: *Great power of Starfyre, forces of Starfyre, Light Rays of Azure Blue. Heal my mind with your calming powers. Heal my body with your soothing powers. Heal my spirit with your tranquil powers. Cause all conflict in my being to cease to be. May peace be radiated from me.*
6. Feel the azure blue light ray energy coming to an apex above your head, swirling about to form a crown.
7. Exhale the azure blue light ray energy and allow it to permeate your auric field and project back into the ambient area.

## ASTRAL ARMOR OF THE BLUE FLAME

Ask/Call forth from the Universal Consciousness the energy vibration/current-ray of Marduk's "*Astral Armor of the Blue Flame*." Visualize the "blue flame" as a protective surface covering your auric-light body and physical body. Charge the armor with the intention to filter all negative/destructive energies encountered and transform them into a positive/constructive polarity before allowing it through—and also deflecting any residual that is not properly transformed.

## GOLDEN BLESSINGS

The golden light radiance (ray energy) of *Starfyre* may bring "golden blessings." This is particularly useful for wealth and business affluence. To attract this, you must vibrate the same energy you seek to attract. As with all energetic metaphysics —"like forces attract like forces." To attract a golden life, use the golden rays of *Starfyre* to project golden light into life.

1. Activate the *Inner Temple*.
2. With eyes open, see golden light ray energy all around you.
3. Hold this imagery for at least three minutes and then inhale the energy.
4. Allow it to wash through your entire being.
5. Intone: *I am surrounded by the golden rays of Starfyre— the Rays and I are one. I make them a part of myself—so mote it be.*
6. Vibrate golden light ray energy into your auric field.
7. Practice this several times daily for effectiveness.

## YELLOW LIGHT—CLEAR MIND (FOCUS)

The yellow color band of *Starfyre* rays are used for mental brilliance and stimulation toward clarity and focus. This is especially useful for times when mental/intellectual prowess is most critical.

1. Activate the *Inner Temple.*
2. Create an atmosphere (surrounding room environment) of brilliant yellow light.
3. Inhale this yellow ray energy and light.
4. Fill you body up with the yellow light.
5. Intone: *Yellow Rays of Starfyre, Yellow Rays of Light— bring to me the riches of clear mind and wisdom. Shine onto me your Yellow Rays of mental strength and personal vitality. Fill me with your mana and bright radiance. Bless me with bright radiance. Bless me with clear light and wisdom for right action. So mote it be.*
6. Exhale the yellow rays of light allowing them to permeate your auric field, radiating outward into your surrounding environment.

# THE CRYSTALLINE AWAKENING*

## A NEW ILLUMINATI

Since the dawn of time, the Earth has been graced with our presence—the true *Guardians of the Earth* and stewards of the *Secrets of the Universe*. Sorcerers. Wizards. Mystics. Now is the time for us to emerge and awaken from our hiding places and greet the times. . . being what they are.

The *Sacred Order of the Crystal Dawn*, or rather what it represents, has been dormant for thousands of years, awaiting a time when the "Wizard" might resume a rightful role in contemporary society—and it is a time of awakening where many will again bond together to once again partake in the *Secret Ceremonies* of the Ancient Mystery School. In accordance with the *Great Plan* of a *New Illuminati*, and by supreme permission of the highest, this "Book of the Mysteries" is hereby opened to our initiates.

## CHAPTER DEFINITIONS

The Chapter: Hereby defined as a "fellowship" of members. Individual "chapters" must report to a "Grant Chapter" for their state/region. Only one "Grand Chapter" can operate in a particular state or region as defined by the "Home Office."

---

\* Commissioned in 1999 by the "Second Order" (or "Inner Circle") of the "*Elven Fellowship Circle of Magick*" (EFCOM) in Denver, known briefly as "*The Sacred Order of the Crystal Dawn.*"

**CHAPTER HEIRARCHY**

<u>Neophyte</u>—The *first degree* of the Crystal Dawn/Elven Fellowship is represented by a small green (new growth) diamond (used in alchemical texts to represent the novice or "puffer") on a red triangle (of the flaming spirit).

<u>Entered Apprentice</u>—A *second degree* initiate is allowed the "Awakening" ceremony after making proper study and preparation. The grade is represented by the alchemical sign for salt in blue—which looks like a scarab—(representing union and absolution of opposition) within an orange triangle.

<u>Adept/Apprentice</u>—A *third degree* initiate has demonstrated aptitude in magickal arts, including ceremonial and high magick. The grade is represented by the black and white eclipse sign on a checkered triangle.

<u>Awakened Apprentice</u>—The *fourth degree* of the Crystal Dawn is reserved for initiates of the mystical arts that extend outside contemporary defined boundaries of occult philosophy and ceremony, emphasizing the mind and spirit. The grade is represented by a red androgyne sign on a green triangle.

<u>Master</u>—A *fifth degree* initiate has completed all "educational" degrees preset by the Crystal Dawn. The sign used to represent the grade is a purple all-seeing eye, within a "squared" blue circle, within in a triangle—which is the sign of the *Philosopher's Stone*. [Additional "Wizard" degrees are treated in a separate volume.]


**INITIATION (AND ATTENDANCE)**

Entrance (admittance) to each degree is supplemented by an initiation/installation ceremony that is open to members in good standing that are initiated to an equal degree (or above) to that which the initiate is being installed to.

## GENDER

The *Sacred Order of the Crystal Dawn* is open to initiates of any gender alignment. Although certain services or practices—areas of dressing, &tc.—may be restricted to certain genders at a given time, there is no bias made concerning general membership or abilities within the *Order*.*

## SPONSORSHIP

To be considered for membership (initiation) into a chapter, and each subsequent degree, candidates must be sponsored by "referral" from an existing member in good standing with the *Order*. The sponsor must be present at the time of the initiation or installation ceremony.‡

## NEOPHYTE INITIATION§

A "Magician/Sponsor" leads the blindfolded "Initiate" to the northeast corner of the *Nemeton*, where the Leader—a group founder or other "ceremonial magician" hereafter referred to as the "Guardian of the Grove"—greets them. The "Guardian" stands in wait at the northeast threshold, holding a sword.

> GUARDIAN OF THE GROVE: *Who is it there that you bring here to the very Gates of this sphere most sacred and secret?*

> MAGICIAN/SPONSOR: *A child of Earth and Star seeking entrance—to be set on the path of our mysteries.*

---

\* This is still upheld by the only surviving faction of the *Sacred Order of the Crystal Dawn*, known today as the "*Mardukite Chamberlains*."
‡ This fundamental is still upheld by the "Second Order" or "Inner Circle" of the "*Mardukite Chamberlains*" and "*Council of Nabu-Tutu*."
§ The "Neophyte Initiation" rite is for the same "Outer Circle" degree of the *Crystal Dawn* and *Elven Fellowship Circle of Magick*, excerpted here as it appears in the "*Elvenomicon*" by Joshua Free.

GUARDIAN: *Do you then present this person to the Grove, vouching before us for their conduct and their dedication to our circle and the Elven Ways?*

SPONSOR: *I do. I sponsor this child of Earth and Star, and must take responsibility for them now . They remain in a state of darkness—blinded to the mysteries of our Nemeton.*

GUARDIAN: *Then, as Guardian of this Gateway, I open the Portal to our Sphere—but it is never broken. You may enter this time by the Unspeakable Password.*

The "Magician/Sponsor" guides the "Initiate" to the center of the circle, where they are set before the existing membership of the Grove.

GUARDIAN: *Answer, Initiate. Do you seek entrance into the mysteries of the "Elven Fellowship Circle of Magick"* [or another name for your personal group]?

INITIATE: *I do.*

GUARDIAN: *Answer, Initiate. Do you come here of your own free will, free from the pressures of peers or others and free of ulterior motives?*

INITIATE: *I do.*

GUARDIAN: *And finally, answer, again: Are you willing to swear an oath to the secrecy by the ancient covenant of the Mystic Wizards of the Earth now raised before you, and this Council, and the spirits we have called to our nemeton?*

INITIATE: *I do.*

GUARDIAN: *Kneel and submit yourself to this Elven Council.*

The "Initiate" kneels and the "Guardian of the Grove" begins to encircle them in *deosil* (counter-clockwise) rotation—drawing up the primal energies of the Earth planet.

GUARDIAN: *You are entering deep woods, the Enchanted World of the Elven-Faerie unsolicited. You step foot on the ground held most sacred to the Keepers of the Earth that maintain and celebrate the ancient Ways. Under penalty of death, no mortal shall step foot on our court unbidden, and thus you now render yourself to the mercy of the Court. You enter a place that is not a place in a time apart from time and still you are here.*

*Fear has no place in our world—here in the Otherworld—and it is our will that you should perish from the spear-blades and arrowheads aimed at you by our Elven military as a sentence for such blasphemy. If you bring mortal fear in your heart to our world, you will undoubtedly summon your demise. How do you enter our world, Initiate?*

INITIATE: *With perfect love and perfect trust.*

GUARDIAN: *I ask the Sponsor: has this Initiate been properly prepared? Has s/he completed their Self-Dedication to the Elven Way? Is the Initiate recognized by the Elemental Portal Guardians of the Watchtowers?*

SPONSOR: *They are prepared. They are dedicated. They are recognized by the Elemental Realms.*

GUARDIAN: *We shall find out. May the Source of All Being and Creation grant us protection; and in protection, strength; and in strength, peace; and in peace, understanding; and in understanding, knowledge; and in knowledge, wisdom; and in wisdom, love; and in love, the love of all things; and in the love of all things, the love of the Universe.*

The "Sponsor" summons the "Initiate" up from their knees, guiding them on a cross-quarter Elemental journey before returning the center again. In ancient times, this would have been conducted in a cave or underground labyrinth. This text is read as the "Sponsor" guides them first to the south, as the "Guardian" reads from the center of the circle:

> *In the beginning was the infinite void of Nothing, a canvas with no form, a screen without picture. But then came Light, the Dragon, the Cosmic Law, that which gave all existence its form, waves of potentiality sprawling across the matrix-fabric of the Universe.*

The "Initiate" is brought to the east:

> *When the fires of life burned down to glowing embers, they breathed into existence the Air, the element of knowledge, and the Elven-Ffayrie spirits of the trees and breeze.*

Across to the west:

> *More and more tangible did the formless Spirit of Light become, when the Waters emerged, ripples sent out to every corner of all encompassing sea. But the currents of energy chased one another and became even more solid.*

And, around to the north:

> *The Formless Fire gave birth to Air; the gaseous Air gave way to water. The sea would yield finally to the land, to the Element of Earth, a powerfully strong and stable foundation to hold up the less tangible manifestations. This Earth is home to the planetary spirit of G'ea—and She has had 'Keepers' and 'Guardians' at all times and places to maintain the balance of the Elemental World and thwart all that would cause disharmony on Earth.*

Returning to the center:

> *As you have come to us in the darkness of ignorance, know*

*that we are the 'Keepers of the Earth,' the 'Guardians of the Green World' and 'Scions of the Secret Knowledge' from the ancients. As you emerge, reborn into a realm of Light and enchantment, your existing name is no longer appropriate and is retired at the boundary of the Sacred Grove. We shall know you as* [circle name for Initiate]. *Welcome Elf/Ffayrie Child, Lord/Lady* [n]*.*

The blindfold is removed. Existing members come forth and greet the Initiate, followed by a celebration in their honor.

## AWAKENING CEREMONY (MODERNIZED)

The initiate is placed in a single room that has been cleared of all else but water and a single candle (already lit on their arrival). They are left to themselves—sealed in the room—for a predetermined period of time. No electrical devices or other sources of light are within the room. The *initiate* is then left only to themselves to run out (or flatten) the analytical mind and eventually (hopefully) overcome diverse personality programs. Such "think-tank" practices may first only be allowed for a few hours, then overnight, and eventually a few days.

The power of the Awakening is gained in the silence, and the speech of wisdom found in the silence—the vision and the voice—and eventually the primordial abyss or "Infinity of Nothingness." When used to initiate/install an Entered Apprentice, the leading *Master* opens the door to complete the time period and the *Initiate* is warmly welcomed in embrace. Ancient versions of this rite included use of caves, labyrinth mazes and other ritual extremes not included here. This rite is also used for the installation of an Awakened Apprentice, or else admittance to the "Second Order" or "Inner Circle" of the *Sacred Order of the Crystal Dawn*. A similar self-disciplined self-managed practice may be used at will for an individual's own deprogramming or *defragmentation* exercises as needed.

## APPRENTICE INITIATIONS

The ritual chamber of the chapter is prepared according to the grade of installation. Members stand in a circle nine feet in diameter around the leading *Master*. The *Sponsor* begins as one among them and the *Initiate* is standing outside the door.

GUARD: *Master of the Craft, there is an initiate awaiting entrance into the n. degree of our Sacred Order.*

MASTER: *Who accounts for this candidate?*

SPONSOR: *I do. S/he stands outside the lodge seeking entrance to the n. degree.*

MASTER: *Has the candidate been properly prepared for the n. degree?*

SPONSOR: *They have.*

MASTER: *Has the candidate been properly prepared for this installation ceremony?*

The *Guard* affirms that they will go and attend to the sponsor, making sure that the hands of the *Initiate* are bound behind their back and that they are blindfolded. The *Sponsor* goes to the center of the circle to wait beside the *Master*. Then, the *Guard* knocks on the door in a "1-2-3" sequence—or another specific to the installation grade. After receiving admittance to the chamber, the *Sponsor* goes and takes stewardship of the *Initiate* from the *Guard* and leads them to stand beside them at the center of the circle, in front of the acting *Master*—and the *Guard* remains by the door to the chamber.

MASTER: *Is the initiate properly prepared?*

SPONSOR: *S/he is.*

MASTER: *Then the initiation may commence. Guard, seal the door. Let no one interfere with these operations.*

The *Guard* locks the door to the lodge chamber and then resumes their post nearest it.

MASTER: *We may proceed.*

SPONSOR: *Master of the Craft, it is my honor to present this candidate for installation to the n. degree of our Sacred Order. I petition this council to allow this candidate initiation to the n degree of this lodge, and mark its occasion.*

MASTER: *I address the initiate—What is it that you seek here from us this day (night)?*

INITIATE: [Answers accordingly.]

MASTER: *That's fine—it is with great pleasure then, that we welcome you to the n degree of the Sacred Order of the Crystal Dawn. By the reputation of your sponsor and the recommendations made on your behalf from your brethren in the lodge, we are assured that you are befitting of the n degree of this lodge and that you will understand this sacred trust being bestowed upon you by this fellowship. Is there any reason why you would be unable to submit yourself to the confidence and commitment of the Sacred Order at this time?*

INITIATE: [Answers accordingly.]

MASTER: *Those who come to this fellowship in Self-Honesty seek to be Self-Masters, assisting themselves and others to assist themselves in Path to Ascension. Do you understand what I have just said?*

INITIATE: [Answers accordingly.]

MASTER: *To be an integral part of this Sacred Order is to seek*

*Self-Honesty, Universal Truth, and the power laden in both. We seek to understand the true nature and potential of the Human condition, now waiting to be unlocked within you. You are here this day to reconfirm the Path to Ascension, the quest for potential and the promise of its loftiest uses, affirming that the Divine Spark and power of God is within you—and that Man is not an Animal. Are you able to solidify this commitment here before your brethren?*

INITIATE: [Answers accordingly.]

MASTER: *Some want to watch the things that move. Some want to tear with their teeth and claws. Some go out fighting. Some go out biting. Punishment is sharp and sure for those who act against the Law. A Human is not an Animal. Man is not an Animal. Today, I am the Sayer of the Law. Speak the words and learn the Law—Not to go on all fours; this is the Law.*

ALL: *Not to go on all fours. That is the law.*

MASTER: *Not to tear at plants and trees. This is the law.*

ALL: *Not to tear at plants and trees. That is the law.*

MASTER: *Not to snarl or roar. This is the law.*

ALL: *Not to snarl or roar. That is the law.*

MASTER: *Not to show teeth or fangs. This is the law.*

ALL: *Not to show teeth or fangs. That is the law.*

MASTER: *Not to destroy our possessions and habitats. This is the law.*

ALL: *Not to destroy our possessions and habitats. That is the law.*

MASTER: *Not to kill without thought. This is the law.*

ALL: *Not to kill without thought. That is the law.*

MASTER: *Man is God.*

ALL: *Man is God.*

MASTER: *We are men.*

ALL: *We are men.*

MASTER: *We are gods.*

ALL: *We are gods.*

MASTER: *God is within and as Man.*

ALL: *God is within and as Man.*

MASTER: *Ours is the hand that creates. This is the law.*

ALL: *Ours is the hand that creates. That is the law.*

MASTER: *Ours is the hand that wounds. This is the law.*

ALL: *Ours is the hand that wounds. That is the law.*

MASTER: *Ours is the hand that heals. This is the law.*

ALL: *Ours is the hand that heals. That is the law.*

MASTER: *Ours is the lightning flash. This is the law.*

ALL: *Ours is the lightning flash. That is the law.*

MASTER: *Ours is the deep salty sea. This is the law.*

ALL: *Ours is the deep salty sea. That is the law.*

MASTER: *Ours is the stars in the sky. This is the law.*

ALL: *Ours is the stars in the sky. That is the law.*

MASTER: *Ours is the rulers of the land. This is the law.*

ALL: *Ours is the rulers of the land. That is the law.*

MASTER: *This is what is ours to have. This is what we are.*

ALL: *This is what is ours to have. This is what we are.*

MASTER: *I now address the Initiate—do you hereby pledge yourself to the n degree of the Order?*

INITIATE: [Answers accordingly.]

MASTER: *Do you swear allegiance to the secrecy of the n degree of the Order?*

INITIATE: [Answers accordingly.]

MASTER: *The sponsor may remove the bindings—in doing so, know that you are now unbound to the potential of the n degree, free to pursue its teachings and instruction.*

The *Sponsor* removes the bindings.

MASTER: *The sponsor may remove the blindfold—in doing so, know that you are now seeing the light of our Order's n degree for the first time. With new eyes you are free to see its teachings and the potential within yourself in Self-Honesty. One cannot seek what they cannot see.*

The *Sponsor* removes the blindfold, then shakes their hand in the grip of the degree.

SPONSOR: *I greet you as a free person of the n. degree.*

All *Members* present follow in performing the same gesture, ending with the acting *Master of the Craft.*

MASTER: *I now declare the installation of this candidate to the n. degree as completed. Guard—release the locks on the door. It is finished. So mote it be.*

ALL: *So mote it be.*

### THE RITE OF TRANSCENDENCE
### (INSTALLATION OF A MASTER)
### A CEREMONY OF THE EQUINOX

The "Transcendent Rite of Transformation" is conducted as the highest ceremonial degree initiation of a chapter-lodge. The acting lodge *Master* or *Master of the Craft* is seated in the east. The *Adept* stands in the west, and is the *Master*'s assistant for this rite. The *Priest* (or *Temple Assistant*) stands at the south, and is subordinate assistant to the *Adept*. A *Guard* is positioned at the chamber door. This ritual refers to the *Master-to-be-installed* (or "initiate") as the "*Deacon*," which usually stands between two pillars of extremity (often distinguished as "black" and "white"; "east" and "west"; or "severity" and "mercy." Elemental Tablets are placed at the four quarters of the chamber (and/or "banners" on the walls).

MASTER: *Brothers and sisters of the Second Order of the Crystal Dawn, assist me now in opening the chapter-lodge for the Transcendent Rite of Transformation and the Ceremony of Equinox—(to install our Brother/Sister to Masterhood).*

The *Guard* makes the appropriate knocks, usually 1-1-2-3.

MASTER: *Guard, seal the door to this lodge. Allow no one to interfere with this assembly.*

The *Guard* secures the door, then remains stationed nearest it, giving the appropriate knock and nodding to the *Priest*.

PRIEST—(to Adept): *The ceremonial lodge is now sealed.*

ADEPT—(to Master): *The ceremonial lodge is now sealed.*

MASTER: *Now that the sanctity of our lodge is sealed and secured, we shall activate the Watchtower Formula.*

The "Watchtower Ceremony-Formula" is performed (see page 98) and then the installation rite continues.

MASTER: *Here we stand at the center of the cosmos; at the equinox of the universe; at the threshold of balance between all forces of Nature—and we gather to observe that center; that equinox; that balance—and radiate that Truth from within.—Beltiste. Soi ten cardian. Didomi cathemerios. Phylaxomenen.*

ALL: *Ee Oh Ee-voh-heh. Ah Oh Ee-voh-heh. Ee Oh Ee-voh-heh.*

ADEPT: *Alphito-Baitule Lusia Nonacris. Anna Fearina Salmoana.*

ALL: *Ee Oh Ee-voh-heh. Ah Oh Ee-voh-heh. Ee Oh Ee-voh-heh.*

PRIEST: *Strabloe Athaneatidas ura druei. Tanaous kolabreusomera.*

ALL: *Ee Oh Ee-voh-heh. Ah Oh Ee-voh-heh. Ee Oh Ee-voh-heh.*

DEACON: *Kirkotokous athroize te Mani. Grog-opa gnathoi ruseis iota.*

ALL: *Ee Oh Ee-voh-heh. Ah Oh Ee-voh-heh. Ee Oh Ee-voh-heh.*

MASTER: *Soul of the Golden Star, grant us strength, passion, joy and love. Soul of the Dark Moon, grant us inspiration, intuition, enchantment and knowledge.*

ADEPT: *Let the Crystalline Pillar shine brightly in our hearts to balance the core of our being, to focus our powers and radiate clear wisdom throughout the unvierse.*

PRIEST: *As we manifest our world of forms and solids, let the clear radiance of the Crystal Dawn bring our spirits renewed Awakening and advancement on the Path to Ascension.*

DEACON/INITIATE: *I am the black pillar. I am the white pillar. I am the reconciliation between them. I am the Fire—Chokmah—Yod. I am the Water—Binah—Heh. I am the Air—Tiphareth-Vahv. I am the Earth—Malkuth-Heh. I am the Universe—An-Ki. I am the Sacred Temple. I am the Priest. I am the Prayer. I am the Receiving Ear. I am the promise fulfilled. I stand before my brethren in Self-Honesty, standing equal among you—a council of gods.*

ADEPT: *In the name of the Divine Breath—IAO—I call forth the spirit of n. to lay thy invisible hand upon our heads and bare witness to this, our solemn oath to the Ascending Light.*

PRIEST: *We call on the aid, protection and guidance by the name and glory of the Tetragrammaton—and by every unspeakable name and unknowable number of God.*

MASTER: *I call forth the Secret Brotherhood in spirit, you who are wise and merciful and who exist without end, for thy have no beginning in this realm. May we enter the abode and sanctuary of thy mysteries. Open the gates of your understanding. Teach us, guide us, and let thy gnosis descend upon us (especially our Brother/Sister n. that is receiving the grace of your Clear Light for the first time).*

The *Master* and *Deacon* approach the Eastern Tablet/Banner.

MASTER: *By the ancient names and signs of the Creators, by the spirit whose name is called Raphael and the Great King of the Eastern Watchtower, Bahtaheevah, behold and adore your Creator. In the name of the Divine Breath: Yod-Heh-Vahv-Heh.*

DEACON: *Yod-Heh-Vahv-Heh.*

The *Adept* (joins) approaches the Eastern Tablet/Banner.

ADEPT: *In and by the name of the Divine Breath: IAO.*

DEACON: *Ee-Ah-Oh.*

The *Priest* (joins) approaches the Eastern Tablet/Banner.

PRIEST: *In and by the secret name Shahdye El Chye.*

DEACON: *Shahdye El Chye.*

MASTER: *I summon ye dwellers of the Eastern realm; kingdom of air; Watchtower of the Dawn—fashion and strengthen the powerful foundation of Astral Light within and as our true selves, that we may render our bodies transformed and approving to the transcendent Invisible Brotherhood.*

When used as an installation ceremony, the *Deacon* speaks the Third Enochian Key (*see page 112*)—otherwise it is spoken by the acting *Master of the Craft.*

MASTER: *Etzarpeh.*

ALL: *Etzarpeh.*

MASTER: *I invoke thee who are crossed by the stars; who are clad by the rays of the Sun; who are the foundation of the universe; who put Comic Law in motion. Look upon this ceremony favorably. Let your rays of Ascending Light descend on us and Awaken our spirit to the Great Work. Yod-Heh-Vahv-Heh.*

ALL: *Yod-Heh-Vahv-Heh.*

ADEPT: *Ee-Ah-Oh.*

ALL: *Ee-Ah-Oh.*

PRIEST: *Shahdye el Chye.*

ALL: *Shahdye el Chye.*

MASTER: *Shemhamphorash.*

ALL: *Shemhamphorash.*

MASTER: *In the names and powers summoned this day, I request the Divine Radiance of Clear Astral Light to descend upon us here and now to transform our corruption into purity; to replace our mortality with divinity; to replace all darkness with the Supernal Light, increasing all life, energy, health and vitality; strengthening the heart, mind, spirit; using the true magic to transfigure our essence into Truth, in perfection with the cosmos. So mote it be.*

ALL: *So mote it be.*

MASTER: *In the true name of the Most High; the spirit of creation; the spirit of the universe—I dispel thee spirits here bound by this ceremony to return to thy place of dwelling in peace. Depart with the blessings of this most Sacred Order and remember.*

ADEPT: *Now that the lodge is to be opened, let this ceremony be closed by the Rite of the Pentagram.*

When used as an installation ceremony, the *Deacon* performs the "Lesser Banishing Ritual of the Pentagram" (*see page 96*)—otherwise it is usually performed by the acting *Master*.

## LAW OF THE MIND

Shakespeare wrote that "...nothing is good or bad except that thinking makes it so." Buddha said "all that we are is the result of what we have thought." And other philosophers have gone forth to speculate how "our life is as our thoughts have made it"—and "action follows thought."

The Law-of-the-Mind is none other than that:—*We Are as we Think we Are to the extent that we Will ourselves to Be.*

Humans have the ability to "create"—they make visible what is only thought of; they enact change; they move energy. Our thoughts and actions can easily be seen as having this ability: to heal, help, harm or destroy. And everything we do either brings us forward or backward in our evolution; everything we do—everything we manifest outwardly—is a reflection of what is held within, because there is no separation of the two.

A fairly common method of employing the "Law of the Mind" is the use of affirmations and mantras. This is not the same as simply "positive thinking" or "wishful thinking"—in fact, we have found that it is not an aspect of "thinking" at all, but is the fact of things or the Laws which "thinking" must obey. It is instead a matter of "willing" the states or conditions of existence and the energetic changes therein. When we see the difference in the statements, it is a bit clearer in description.

| | |
|---|---|
| (Thinking) | *I want* to be a better person. |
| (Willing) | *I am* a success in what I think and do. |
| | |
| (Thinking) | *I wish* I were feeling better. |
| (Willing) | *I am* vibrant with good health. |

Your mind is programmed to display what it "knows" or has been "taught"—to the extent you can understand—but this state of knowingness is also under the control of your "Will," whether or not you maintain proper control over it.

Reality is reinforced everyday by your agreements with the predilections of said reality. But, you do not actually have to agree with what you are programmed to see. You can change what you are seeing and why you are seeing it. Any of these changes on a physical level may seem superficial—only lending to further various personality programming—but there is a deeper level to these "outward occult" demonstrations; or else, "there is a magic behind the magic," which promotes an increased awareness, consciousness-shifts and upgrades for the human condition that advance a true spiritual evolution *Crystal Clear* in *Self-Honesty*. Walter Silverton wrote that "our life is just like a mirror." NexGen Systemology describes it as a "crystal" or lens. We observe situations and conditions taking form exactly according to the thoughts we are constantly projecting from the *Self* into the "creative mind."

## CONDITIONS OF EXISTENCE

There are three conditions of existence which are: to *be*, to *do* and to *have*, which correspond to the states of *beingness*, of *doingness* and of *havingness*.

---

—The condition of *being* is the assuming of the identity of one's physical characteristics.

—The condition of *doing* is the accomplishment of goals and fulfillment of one's personal/individual purpose.

—The condition of *having* is the ability to command or else take charge of the energy and space.

---

People assume identity programs that can may them attention, but they may be feeding all of the their energy toward *being*—and thereby never enter conditions of *doing* and states of *havingness*. Without responsibility there is no power, there is simply *beingness*. Those who do not self-actualize their own identity programs will criticize others to achieve *havingness*.

## DETERMINATION

There are two types of determinism that apply to the current curriculum. *Self-Determinism* is the personal power over the Will to successfully accomplish a mission or task—this is *self-mastery*. Pan-Determinism is the ability to engineer Reality as experienced by others. *Self-Determinism* requires strengthening of the Will and conscious control of the Mind and Laws of the Mind from and as *Self*. To extend this Reality to others, in turn, requires abilities to consciously project communicable energies into a group consciousness or "the Group Mind."

## NEXGEN SYSTEMOLOGY—THE NEW AWAKENING

The *Alpha Spirit* is multifaceted—in possession of a *human genetic vehicle* pertaining to a Body, Mind and Spirit ("Divine Spark") operating as a single "identity." Each co-exists with the others at a specific existential degree of the Human Condition—the Mind is able to see them as separate and manifold—and the Spirit is able to see the workings of the Mind having an effect with the Body. This Spirit is the "god-in-man" that is actually *doing* the reality creating and *seeing* it beyond the experiences of the analytical Mind. We merely must shift our total Awareness into *Spirit*.

The *Mind* is the communication center between the Spirit and the functions of the Body—including all psychosomatic results and emotional/chemical/hormonal productions. It is this communication relay that allows us to "interpret" our environment via sensory stimuli. The Mind is constantly calculating and factoring the data that the Body receives. Highest degrees of the *Sacred Order of the Crystal Dawn* are most concerned with the *Mind* and *Knowingness*. By better understanding the Mind, we have a better clearer avenue open to us by which we might be able to later explore the nature and abilities of the *Spirit* in *Self-Honesty*.

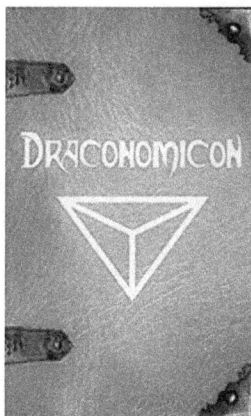

**DRACONOMICON**
The Book of Ancient Dragon Magick
25th Anniversary Collector's Edition
*by Joshua Free*

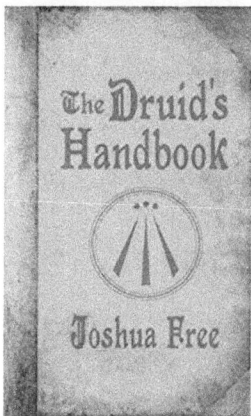

**THE DRUID'S HANDBOOK**
Ancient Magick for a New Age
20th Anniversary Collector's Edition
*by Joshua Free*

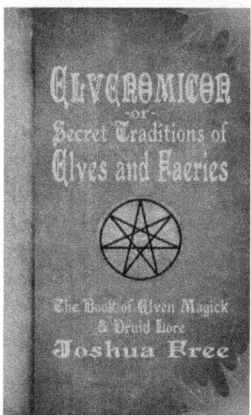

**ELVENOMICON -or-**
**SECRET TRADITIONS OF**
**ELVES AND FAERIES**
The Book of Elven Magick
& Druid Lore
15th Anniversary Collector's Edition
*by Joshua Free*

*Necronomicon: The Anunnaki Bible* : 10th Anniversary
  Collector's Edition—LIBER-N,L,G,9+W-M+S  (*Hardcover*)

*The Complete Anunnaki Bible: A Source Book of Esoteric Archaeology* :
  10th Anniversary—LIBER-N,L,G,9+W-M+S (*Paperback*)

*Necronomicon: The Anunnaki Bible* : 10th Anniversary
  Pocket Edition—(*Abridged Paperback*)

*Gates of the Necronomicon: The Secret Anunnaki Tradition of
  Babylon* : 10th Anniversary Collector's Edition—
  LIBER-50,51/52,R+555  (*Hardcover*)

*The Sumerian Legacy: A Guide to Esoteric Archaeology*—
  LIBER-50+51/52  (*Paperback*)

*Necronomicon Revelations—Crossing to the Abyss: Nine Gates
  of the Kingdom of Shadows & Simon's Necronomicon*—
  LIBER-R+555  (*Paperback*)

*Necronomicon: The Anunnaki Grimoire: A Manual of Practical
  Babylonian Magick* : 10th Anniversary Collector's Edition—
  LIBER-E,W/Z,M+K  (*Hardcover*)

*Practical Babylonian Magic : Invoking the Power of the Sumerian
  Anunnaki*—LIBER-E,W/Z,M+K (*Paperback*)

*The Complete Book of Marduk by Nabu : A Pocket Anunnaki
  Devotional Companion to Babylonian Prayers & Rituals* :
    10th Anniversary Collector's Edition—LIBER-W+Z (*Hardcover*)

*The Maqlu Ritual Book : A Pocket Companion to Babylonian
  Exorcisms, Banishing Rites & Protective Spells* :
    10th Anniversary Collector's Edition—LIBER-M  (*Hardcover*)

*Necronomicon: The Anunnaki Spellbook* : 10th Anniversary
  Pocket Edition—LIBER-W/Z+M  (*Abridged Paperback*)

*The Anunnaki Tarot : Consulting the Babylonian Oracle of
  Cosmic Wisdom (Guide Book)*—LIBER-T  (*Paperback*)

*Elvenomicon—Secret Traditions of Elves & Faeries : The Book of
  Elven Magick & Druid Lore :* 15th Anniversary Collector's
  Edition—LIBER-D  (*Hardcover*)

*The Druid's Handbook : Ancient Magick for a New Age*
  20th Anniversary Collector's Edition—LIBER-D2  (*Hardcover*)

*Draconomicon : The Book of Ancient Dragon Magick :*
  25th Anniversary Collector's Edition—LIBER-D3  (*Hardcover*)

*The Sorcerer's Handbook : A Complete Guide to Practical Magick*
  21st Anniversary Collector's Edition—(*Hardcover*)

NABU—JOSHUA FREE ("Merlyn Stone")
Chief Scribe & Librarian of New Babylon
Bard of the Twelfth Chair at New Forest